Back in the Saddle Again

How to Overcome Fear of Riding After a Motorcycle Accident

Brenda L. Bates, MA, CHt.

Second Edition

Bike Psych
PUBLISHING

Sutherlin, Oregon

First Edition 2006
Brenda Leigh Bates   Self published e book
Bates Counseling and Hypnosis
www.bikepsych.com
Edited by Lisa S. Childs

Second Edition Revised 2009
Bike Psych Publishing
Copy Editing by Jennifer Ward
Cover Art and Design by John P. Kaufman

Copyright © 2002, 2009 by Brenda Leigh Bates

ISBN: 978-0-578-00614-7   (pbk)

Library of Congress Control Number: 2007930146

Library of Congress Cataloging in Publication Data:
Bates, Brenda Leigh
    Back in the Saddle Again: How to Overcome Fear of Riding
    After a Motorcycle Accident / Brenda Leigh Bates / 2002-08-23
    1 v.

Dedication

To my father and mother. May they rest in peace and in love.

Special Thanks
To my editors, L.S. Childs and J. Ward.

Brenda, age 12, with mother, Barbara J. Hilyer-Bates.

Brenda's father, G.W. Bates.

All examples used in this book are fiction. Any resemblance to persons living or dead is coincidental.

Contents

Foreword

This book is for the motorcyclist who has been in an accident. Whether you were involved in a traumatic motorcycle accident or you are experiencing indirect emotional trauma due to the accident of a friend or loved one, this book is for you.

Before your accident, you may have ridden on- or off-road. You may have ridden primarily as a passenger. You may have raced on the professional or amateur circuit. You may be male or female. Whatever the case may be, if you consider yourself to be a motorcyclist and have been in an accident, this book is dedicated to you.

Moreover, it is my hope that this book will prove illuminating to motorcyclists who have not been involved in an accident but who find it beneficial, rewarding, and interesting to learn about the psychology of motorcyclists. *Back in the Saddle Again* is a first-of-its-kind study into the minds of motorcyclists. This book can also be a powerful and useful guide to help you to manage any fears or anxieties you may have around riding. *Back in the Saddle Again* can also help those who are assisting and supporting post-accident motorcyclists by clarifying the issues that the rider is experiencing internally.

The clinical diagnosis for someone involved in a traumatic accident is often post traumatic stress disorder (PTSD). For the motorcyclist, the emotional effects of PSTD can be devastating. Motorcyclists with PTSD often feel that they have been left with invisible emotional scars that linger on long after the physical wounds have healed. These invisible scars can cause the motorcyclist to experience a whirlwind of emotions.

Often scary, confusing, ambivalent, disquieting, and even embarrassing, these emotions can leave the motorcyclist feeling unable to explain to others the turmoil felt within. And perhaps worst of all, a motorcyclist with PTSD will typically find him or herself avoiding the very thing they once longed for—riding a motorcycle.

This book is designed to point the motorcyclist who is considering riding again toward the road to recovery. This road is not always an easy one; at times it can be riddled with obstacles. I have mapped out *Back in the Saddle Again* to help you successfully navigate these psychological obstacles. Each chapter is intended to clarify the emotional roadblocks that you have been experiencing which prevent you from enjoying your motorcycle.

With the aid of this book, you will learn how to recognize the symptoms of PTSD, and you will learn how to manage them. You will discover common, psychological issues motorcyclists are often confronted with after an accident. Through case examples, you will become familiar with others who have been in the same psychological state. And should you decide that you want to continue to ride, this book will help you to get "back in the saddle again."

So without further hesitation, open your mind to full throttle, and meet me at our first stop: Chapter One.

CHAPTER 1

Post Traumatic Stress Disorder

A split second of terrifying realization—the sound of screeching tires—a brief sensation of falling or being thrown—and it's all over. Sound familiar? Next comes the trip to the hospital emergency room. For some, this trip is only the beginning of a long hospital stay, followed by a lengthy treatment process including physical therapy. For others, the emergency room is a relatively brief encounter. These more fortunate victims of a motorcycle accident may be sent home the same day with casts, stitches, or bandages. Whether the injuries you incurred were serious or comparatively minor, you may have found you have emotional wounds that have gone untreated by all of the x-rays and bandages.

Perhaps your motorcycle accident was the first one. Perhaps it is only one in a series. Maybe you were involved in a collision with an automobile, another motorcycle, or a bicycle. Or you may have collided with an animal or experienced a single-vehicle accident in which you were the only living being involved. Whatever the case may be, you could suddenly find yourself in the grips of PTSD.

According to the *Diagnostic and Statistical Manual of Mental Disorders IV, Ed.* (the diagnostic manual used by all American mental health professionals, published by the American Psychiatric Association, Inc.), PTSD involves a cluster of symptoms including, but not limited to the following:

1. A frequent sense that you are reliving the trauma. Accompanying this may be flashbacks of the event, which may include hallucinations or intrusive internal visualizations/memories. Often flashbacks occur with a feeling that you are emotionally reliving the trauma.

2. The experience of recurring nightmares or "daymares" of the trauma.

3. Intrusive memories and images of the trauma that seem to haunt you wherever you go.

4. Intense distress over anything resembling the trauma.

5. Avoidance of things, places, situations, and/or people that remind you of the trauma.

6. A numbing effect in which you seem to be absent of feelings, particularly, but not necessarily only, around anything to do with the trauma.

7. Changes in your sleeping patterns.

8. Changes in eating patterns.

You do not have to be experiencing all of these symptoms to be diagnosed with PTSD. However, if you've been involved in a trauma, you may likely experience a few of these symptoms. Even a few symptoms are enough to warrant the utilization of this book. It's best to manage your symptoms now so that they do not begin to spill over into other areas of your life.

Different resources, new research, and various clinicians sometimes disagree upon the number of symptoms a person should have in order to be diagnosed with PTSD. Some of the suggestions in this chapter about PTSD have been adapted from the book, *Post-Traumatic Stress Disorder: The Latest Assessment and Treatment Strategies* (Friedman, Mathew J., M.D., Ph.D., Kansas City, MO: Dean Psych Press Corp, 2000.) In my professional opinion, three or more symptoms usually warrant the diagnosis, provided that at the time of the incident

1. You experienced, witnessed, or in some way had to deal with a potentially life-threatening trauma that involved or threatened death or serious physical injury to you or someone close to you. Or that you were witness to such a trauma to individual(s) unknown to you.

2. You responded to the trauma with a feeling of helplessness, fear, or horror.

It is not uncommon for PTSD symptoms to slip over into areas of your life that are not even related to motorcycling. For example, some people may find that they begin to experience a numbing and/or debilitating feeling around many things in life—for example, work and personal relationships.

Often those who have gone without psychological treatment of some kind can have symptoms of PTSD for years. Often these people have an exaggerated startle response; they are nervous and jumpy over the slightest little thing. In fact, research shows that left untreated, some individuals may never recover from PTSD. (Research of Nazi Holocaust survivors shows that PTSD can endure for a lifetime.)

Statistically, PTSD is considered a public mental health problem affecting millions of Americans. It is estimated that 8 percent of Americans will develop PTSD at some point in their life. Predisposing factors for the development of PTSD include the following: the experience of childhood trauma; poor health; financial problems; and/or the recent experience of adverse life events, such as divorce and loss of job. And, generally speaking, the greater the trauma, the greater the tendency to develop PTSD.

PTSD can occur within a month after the trauma, or it can suddenly arise up to six months after the incident. For motorcyclists, avoiding motorcycles or situations that involve motorcycles and avoiding riding itself are all common symptoms of PTSD. The degree to which you are experiencing avoidance behaviors is in direct relationship to the severity of your PTSD.

Some individuals find that they are still able to be around motorcycles and even to ride. However, if this is you, you are probably experiencing some degree of avoidance and anxiety around the act of riding. Perhaps you find yourself avoiding roads that remind you of your accident. Perhaps you find you can no longer keep up with traffic. Perhaps you have found yourself riding along and suddenly becoming overwhelmed, gripping the handlebars as your heart pounds rapidly. On the other hand, many post-accident motorcyclists find that they can't even look at motorcycles without feeling fearful or numb.

Often, but not always, motorcyclists with severe PTSD may have virtually no memories of their trauma for weeks, months, or even years after the accident. For some, these memories do eventually emerge. This blocking of the traumatic memory is a psychological protective mechanism. It serves to shield the motorcyclist from memories that are too overwhelming to face.

Likewise, a person who has been seriously injured in an accident but remained conscious may be unaware of any bodily pain. This numbing of pain may be psychosomatic in origin, meaning it is caused by emotional shock. Some post-accident riders don't bother to go to a hospital due to lack of pain. But pain or not, it is important that the rider does go for a medical exam just in case the lack of pain is psychosomatic in origin.

Recovering memories of the trauma is not a necessity. Sometimes these cognitive blocks dissolve over time. But it is important to realize that even if the memories are never recovered, psychological healing can still take place by dealing with the presenting symptoms. Be wary of using hypnosis or other means to recover memories of trauma. Studies show that our memories can be unreliable. Fact, fantasy, and symbolism can be mixed together, creating what is known as "false memory syndrome." Don't push yourself to remember what your mind is trying to protect from your conscious awareness.

Although there is often a connection between the severity of the accident and the severity of PTSD symptoms, some individuals can develop severe PTSD as a result of a minor accident with minor injuries. This is due to the psychological makeup of the individual prior to the accident. Factors such as past traumas, psychological coping skills, and social support can all influence the degree to which an individual may experience PTSD as a result of an accident.

For individuals who develop severe PTSD (three or more symptoms that are significantly interfering with the individual's life) without having suffered serious physical injury, it is important to realize that emotional trauma, in its own right, can be just as debilitating as physical trauma. Be careful not to buy into the "just get over it" motto. This motto is nothing but snake oil: It doesn't work, never has, and never will. *Back in the Saddle Again* will help you to sort through what you are feeling so that you will be better equipped to manage these feelings.

Another factor which can influence the development

of severe PTSD is the belief or knowledge that another person maliciously intended to cause you to have an accident. PTSD may be less severe if you were involved in a single vehicle accident that was not caused by anyone else. Also, some studies indicate that psychological treatment soon after the accident decreases the risk of developing PTSD. The chapter on debriefing in this book is designed to help with this.

Useful treatment modalities for motorcyclists with PTSD include

1. Cognitive/behavioral techniques (as described later in this book).

2. Hypnosis (also described later in this book).

3. Medically-prescribed psychiatric medications.

4. Educating oneself about the emotional and psychological issues that occur after a motorcycle accident and taking self-directed steps to utilize the psychological information and recovery techniques presented in this book.

5. Getting yourself hooked up with a social support network.

Certain individuals require the use of all five techniques in order to recover from PTSD. However, often the use of cognitive/behavioral techniques and/or *properly* using hypnosis will lead to recovery. For some, simply learning about the psychological issues is enough to help move through them. For these people, education, clarification, and demystification are enough to enable them to self-manage their own psychological recovery. *Back in the Saddle Again* was written to assist you in this way.

If you and your doctor determine that it would be in your own best interest to try a prescribed medication for

PTSD, there is no sound reason not to try this. For individuals who decide to take a prescribed medication, it is important that they do not do so to the exclusion of psychological, hypnotic, and/or educational interventions. This is because it is necessary to develop new psychological coping strategies so that you do not run the risk of your symptoms recurring once you stop taking the medication. If you and your doctor determine that trying prescribed medication for emotional distress or anxiety is in your best interest, then educate yourself about these medications and try not to allow the "social stigma" surrounding medication to interfere with your decision.

While many people don't like the idea of taking a psychiatric medication, it is important to realize that these medications are designed to interact with your brain in a positive way. Anti-depressant or anti-anxiety medications will not change your personality. If taken as prescribed, they will not harm you. What they will do is lift the cloud that sometimes hovers around the post-accident motorcyclist, thereby expediting psychological recovery. It may be helpful to realize that all of our perceptions are in some way affected by chemical reactions in the brain. Therefore, taking a prescribed medication is nothing more than capitalizing on the brain's own natural chemistry.

PTSD is currently thought of by many in the mental health fields as a normal reaction to an abnormal situation. As mentioned earlier, being in an accident doesn't absolutely mean that you will develop PTSD. However, you will likely experience at least some anxiety related to PTSD symptoms.

The mental health community has gained much insight into the diagnosis and treatment of PTSD in recent years. Around the turn of twentieth century, medical professionals called what we now know as PTSD, "hysteria." They tended to believe that hysteria primarily affected females and was caused by the uterus. While this is a silly notion now, at that time Western medicine understood next to nothing about oppression, rape, and childhood molestation, which many women who were labeled as hysterics had suffered. Women who suffered from hysteria were frequently seen by the medical community, because there was no place else for them to turn. During that time, psychological counseling as we know it today was in its infancy.

With the occurrence of WWI, and more specifically WWII, the medical community began to see symptoms previously diagnosed as hysteria in returning veterans. Since these veterans were largely men, the medical community realized that a uterus couldn't possibly be the cause of such symptoms. So the diagnosis was changed to "shell shock." During and after the Vietnam War, shell-shocked vets were again seen in large numbers. The diagnosis of shell shock was then changed to "combat fatigue." Today, the terms "hysteria," "shell shock," and "combat fatigue" are no longer used. Post traumatic stress disorder is now the official diagnosis.

Although PTSD has always existed, it wasn't until 1980 when it was formally identified in the mental health and medical communities. We now know that PTSD is caused by psychological trauma and does not discriminate between the sexes.

CHAPTER 2

Individual Identity and Motorcycles

Deciding to ride again after a traumatic accident is a personal decision. Ultimately, it is a decision that should orbit around your sense of individual identity. Deciding to ride again or not should be a self-directed choice and not a trauma-directed one. In this way, you will be better able to maintain your sense of personal integrity.

Often, post-accident motorcyclists feel torn between wondering if riding is worth the risk any more and that old feeling of what can be best described as "bike-passion." This ambivalence is largely due to the traumatic feelings of helplessness and fear that are common symptoms of PTSD. By helplessness, I mean that you probably feel that you no longer possess that certain "in control" sense to manage your own safety.

If you decide that you do want to ride again, you need to develop a plan to minimize future riding risks. Planning is actually a psychological coping strategy that includes weighing benefits against risks, with consideration to potentially positive and negative consequences. Even if before your accident you had a strategy, nothing is set in stone. One can always benefit by reevaluating what risk-reducing behaviors you may have had and then deciding which ones to keep and which new ones to add.

By reading this book, you are showing that you are ready to take certain steps in this direction. If you have never taken a motorcycle safety course, or even if you have, now is a good time to consider taking one. You may even want to consider taking a formal track class. These classes put one in an environment larger than a parking lot and are more akin to an actual road environment. Not only will taking a course improve your riding skills; it will also help you to regain your sense of mastery. By regaining your sense of mastery, you will be directly combating your feelings of helplessness. Simultaneously, your brain will develop neural pathways to help you to learn to ride anew.

Neural pathways in the brain can be likened to tracts that are present in the brain tissue. It is theorized that the mind refers to these tracts in order to know how to conduct itself in a given situation. It stands to reason then, that trauma and all its associated symptoms, such as panic, fear, etc. build their own tracts in the brain. This being so, it would be a bad thing for an individual's brain to rely upon trauma-created tracts. If that individual is about to ride again, it is psychologically and biochemically sound to develop new, healthy tracts created by good riding skills and sound judgment. After all, riding again after an accident is, in many ways, like taking up riding for the first time.

Additionally, read books written by the experts on how to ride properly and minimize risks. Not only will these books help you with new skills; they will also serve as a psychological first step toward getting "back in the saddle again." (This is in no way to imply that your skills were wrong or bad before your accident. Rather, it is a psychological step in the right direction toward combating your anxieties.)

Your decision to ride again or not will ultimately rest upon whether being a motorcyclist is an important part of your identity. To help you to discover this, I have developed a psychological questionnaire specifically for motorcyclists.

11 WAYS TO KNOW IF BEING A MOTORCYCLIST IS AN IMPORTANT PART OF YOUR IDENTITY

Answer "Yes" or "No" to each of the following statements:

1. You have been involved in social events that revolve around riding.

   Or, if you have not done so, you would very much have liked to attend such events. This is known as ceremonial riding.

2. You have felt a need to connect with other riders—even if only through reading-related material.

3. Being a motorcyclist has given you a feeling of being special or unique.

4. You have named your motorcycle, or you refer to it as "he or "she."

5. You have customized or otherwise personalized your bike.

6. Much of your free time has involved thoughts of riding and/or planning rides.

7. You have supported riding (or really wanted to) even in the company of those who are against it.

8. You have been interested in the laws concerning motorcycles and riding (for example, helmet laws).

9. You have invested money into motorcycling-related items (such as clothing and memorabilia).

10. You have rewarded yourself by going for a ride or through motorcycling-related activities.

11. Riding is the best (or only) activity that you know that helps you to relieve stress, and/or if you don't ride for a period of time, you feel a certain buildup of tension. In psychodynamic terms this is connected to the libidinous aspect of life's energy.

If you have answered "Yes" to six or more of these queries, then chances are that being a motorcyclist IS an important part of your identity.

11 WAYS TO KNOW IF BEING A MOTORCYCLIST IS *NOT* AN IMPORTANT PART OF YOUR IDENTITY

Answer "Yes" or "No" to each of the following statements:

1. A motorcycle is primarily a form of cheap transportation.

2. You would prefer to own a special or exotic automobile rather than a motorcycle.

3. In the past five years you have had a fluctuating interest in motorcycles and riding. You have and can easily transfer your interest in motorcycles to another activity.

4. You have been involved in, or are aware of, at least one other activity that you find just as, or even more fulfilling, than motorcycling.

5. You have not had an interest in supporting riding in the company of those who are against it.

6. Your motorcycle battery has occasionally gone dead from nonuse, and/or you have taken little interest in the proper maintenance of your bike. For example, you're not sure when your oil was last changed.

7. You do not own or have any particular desire to own any special riding attire other than what is required by law (attire may be safety or fashion oriented).

8. The appearance and/or brand of your motorcycle do not really interest you.

9. You have not had a desire to be connected with other riders, i.e. through having riding friends, attending social events, or through magazines and books.

10. You can virtually forget about motorcycles and riding for months at a time.

11. You wouldn't spend your hard-earned cash on motorcycle magazine subscriptions, books, memorabilia, or events.

If you have answered "Yes" to six or more of these queries, then chances are being a motorcyclist is NOT an important part of your identity.

Nonetheless, if you still feel that something is missing from your life without bikes, then try some sort of motorcycling-related involvement that does not include actually riding. Go to the races, for example, or attend local bike shows. You may find that this is enough to satisfy you. Moreover, some riders who really want to ride again but find the fear too overwhelming may find that attending motorcycling activities without actually riding can be a helpful step toward getting "back in the saddle again."

While this test should not be thought of as an absolute, your answers provide a good indication as to whether or not taking up riding again is in your best interest.

Let's look at two case examples that describe one individual from the "identity" category and one from the "Not Part Of Identity" category. See if you can identify the statements that reveal each individual's identity status concerning motorcycles.

CASE EXAMPLE #1

Bradford, a 44-year-old family man and business attorney, was involved in a motorcycle accident that was caused by a drunk automobile driver. Bradford's physical injuries included the amputation of his left leg below the knee. Here is his story:

"After my accident, I began to wonder if I wasn't kidding myself over this whole motorcycle thing. I began to wonder if I wasn't being selfish and irresponsible by riding motorcycles. I started avoiding going into my garage where I kept my vintage bike collection. My friends from the vintage club sent me get-well cards and kept calling me on the phone. I always loved these people, but somehow I kept making excuses as to why I couldn't see or talk to them. Then I started looking at my wife and kids as though I'd never see them again if I decided to get back to riding. My partners from the office were calling me almost everyday. People needed me, you know? I was thinking that I was taking unnecessary risks by riding. Worse than that, I felt as if I were some kind of a joke. What's a middle-aged man doing with all of these bikes anyway? Then I questioned my ability to ever ride safely again. I was convincing myself that my reflexes weren't what they used to be—that I wasn't as strong as I used to be. Heck, I wasn't even a whole man any more! I really started to hit bottom when I began to think that I was altogether incompetent as a man. I was just a helpless old fool. One day I forced myself to go into my garage and price all of my girls (referring to motorcycles), riding gear, and vintage memorabilia. I was going to sell everything. Suddenly, I was struck by two opposing feelings. Part of me felt that awful anxiety over the thought of ever riding again; the other part of me was hit by my old passion for these vintage dream-machines. This is when things started to turn around for me. I decided to get help and learned that I had post traumatic stress disorder. I learned that I could be taught to manage my symptoms. Soon I found myself daydreaming again about riding. I even began to plan some of the rides I hadn't yet experienced. After I had been back to work for awhile, I realized how much I needed to ride again. I really believe it's the one thing that has stood between me and that ulcer so many of my colleagues have. For me, riding is like a reward. I've tried other things, too. My wife and I took scuba diving and surfing lessons once. These things are fun, but I guess I've always known that nothing hits the spot for me like motorcycles. A few fellows at work can't believe that I didn't sell all my bikes. They think I have a secret death wish and that I'm crazy that way. I just tell them, "I may be crazy, but at least I have something that works for me. All you have is an ulcer."

Were you able to identify Bradford's statements that serve as clues that motorcycling is an important part of his identity? Can you read Bradford's story again and count these clues? What in Bradford's story revealed his PTSD symptoms? Remember, these are the statements that express his avoidance behaviors, feelings of helplessness, fear, and anxiety around riding. See if you can identify and count these clues as you reread Bradford's comments.

Since Bradford's sense of identity does include being a motorcyclist, it is not surprising that he did decide to ride again. His first day out was on his yellow Laverda Jota.

CASE EXAMPLE #2

When Bob initially came to see me for therapy, he was a 25-year-old graduate student. The night of his accident, Bob was riding home from a party where he had consumed quite a lot of beer. He ran into a parked car at about 40 mph.

The result of this accident for Bob was a broken collarbone and cracked ribs. Here is his story:

"If there's anything I can't stand, it's being controlled by fear. I do not want to live my life being afraid of motorcycles or anything else. After my accident, I was only afraid of motorcycles; that was bad enough. Then about six months later I found myself being afraid of anything that involved even the smallest risk. Like, I want to join my school's wrestling team. Now, that's even more challenging than bikes! Problem is, I'm having all sorts of anxiety over even doing that. I remember when I was a kid, and I got a chance to see that *Easy Rider* movie with some buddies of mine. I know it sounds totally stupid, but for months after that I dreamed of growing up and being just like Peter Fonda. Eventually I got involved with wrestling and forgot about bikes. Then a couple years ago I needed some cheap transportation. I was just a poor student, so I bought this used dual-purpose bike. One thing great about that bike was that it just ran and ran. I never put a single penny into it except for gas. Anyway, I thought it was really great. I had a lot of fun riding it. Don't laugh, but at first I even remembered about that whole Peter Fonda thing. A couple of close friends who care about me warned me that bikes are dangerous. They said I should just take the bus. I didn't bother to say anything to them at the time 'cause, I don't know, it's not like I was a hard-core biker or anything. I should have listened to them. After my accident I kept hearing their warnings over and over in my head. After my accident, I began to really think about my philosophical position on bikes. I haven't come to a conclusion yet, and I haven't told any of my friends about what I'm thinking. In fact, I usually do anything I can to avoid talking to anyone about bikes. It makes me so nervous, sometimes I begin to sweat. Anyway, I have to say that I really had fun riding. Besides, it's a form of transportation that I can actually afford. I need to decide whether or not to get another bike. I want to make this decision for myself. I refuse to let fear make it for me! If I could just get over my fear, maybe I could enjoy riding again. I'm really not sure what to do. I feel like a "helpless little old lady."

Notice that Bob had at least five statements revealing that being a motorcyclist was not an important part of his identity. As you reread Bob's story, try to identify these statements. Bob decided that, for him, riding simply wasn't worth the risk anymore.

However, Bob still needed to deal with his PTSD. You can tell from Bob's comments that PTSD-related fear and anxiety was spilling over into other areas of his life. Today, Bob is a star on his school's wrestling team. He is also a regular customer on the public transportation system.

Like Bradford and Bob, you, too, need to make a self-directed choice. Ask yourself if your passion for motorcycling overrides the fear. If the answer is "Yes," or a potential "Yes," then you may be deciding that being a motorcyclist is worth the risk. This is not to say that you blindly accept this risk. Rather, you need to develop a plan to minimize future riding risks and to rekindle your sense of mastery. Your plan should include

1. Learning how to manage your PTSD symptoms (detailed later in this book).

2. Developing a network of social support by sharing your concerns with others who have also decided to ride again after an accident.

3. Taking a rider safety or track course.

4. Reading books by experts on proper riding skills.

5. Identifying your limitations.

6. Investing in the best protective riding gear.

7. Paying close attention to the motorcycle manufacturer's recommended service schedule.

8. Some post-accident motorcyclists carry a cell phone and always let someone know exactly where they will be riding that day.

9. Add your own ideas here. Feel free to add to this list as time goes on.

You have now learned a great deal about PTSD. You have also gained food for thought concerning a personalized risk-management plan. All of this knowledge will serve as your foundation as you read the following chapters. Moreover, you now have a keener understanding as to how your individual identity is the key determinant for your choice to ride again. With all this under your belt, you are ready to be introduced to more specific psychological issues commonly experienced by post-accident motorcyclists.

CHAPTER 3

The Existential Motorcyclist

In the German language, the word "zeitgeist" loosely translated means "in the spirit of the times." Zeitgeist describes connections between occurrences and developments that join seemingly unrelated fields or events (Leonard Schlain, *Art and Physics*, New York: William Morrow and Co., 1991). For example, Albert Einstein, who died in 1955, completely revised our notion of space and time. While his Theory of Relativity is difficult to explain, it is perhaps easier to understand in terms of the style of art called, cubism. Relativity and cubism are connected.

Cubism, largely attributed to artists such as Pablo Picasso, exploded into the art scene around the same time as Einstein's Theory of Relativity. Yet Picasso and Einstein lived in two different countries, were in different elements of society, and were unacquainted with one another. Nonetheless, cubistic art is akin to the Theory of Relativity. One may even say that cubism is the material expression for the Theory of Relativity.

Cubism sets time, space, light, and motion in a simultaneous pattern instead of a linear one. This is why a cubist painting may, for example, depict a woman with her breast on her head and her hand where her knee should be. Basically, the viewer is seeing the woman in the painting from all angles at the same time. This makes the painting more than three dimensional, and implies virtually the same concept of time, space and motion as in Einstein's Theory of Relativity. The Cubistic idea is therefore remarkably similar to the concept of relativity; time, space, and motion are overlapping and happening at once.

Cubism was just as revolutionary for the art world of the times as was Einstein's Theory of Relativity to science at that time. Since both concepts are the same in essence, the word "zeitgeist" applies.

Zeitgeist also applies to the advent of the philosophy known as existentialism and the invention of the motorcycle. Existentialism is a philosophy that posits man/woman as alone in a world filled with a myriad of choices. Further, existentialism asserts that life in and of itself has no true meaning. It is up to each individual to take personal responsibility and invest life with meaning for him or herself. On the surface, this concept may appear to negate the idea of a God. However, this is not necessarily the case. One can have religious or spiritual beliefs and still maintain that psychologically we are each responsible for making choices and putting our efforts into a self-directed path. This is free will.

Many consider the founders of existentialism to be Dostoyevsky (1821-1881), a Russian novelist, and Kierkegaard (1813-1855), a Danish philosopher. The first motorcycle to appear publicly was created by Gottlieb Daimler in 1885—hence, "zeitgeist" of a kind.

As with Picasso and Einstein, there is no evidence that existential followers were acquainted with Daimler, or vice-versa. Nevertheless, a relationship was born between the developments. In many ways, the motorcycle was to become the material interpretation of theoretical existentialism.

Exactly how zeitgeist happens (and it has happened countless times in history) may be explained by John Wheeler, who was a student of one of the founders of quantum physics, Niels Bohr. Wheeler expanded on Bohr's theory of a "mind, universe" connection. Wheeler asserted that in a quantum physical way, mind and universe are interrelated and interconnected. This interweave of consciousness and universe is called the theory of "complementarity," which was originated in 1926 by Bohr. Accordingly, all events interconnect on a level of which we are unaware and cannot measure (Shlain, 1991).

During the approximate time of the development of the theory of complementarity, a Swiss psychologist named Carl Jung developed a similar theory called "synchronicity." The theories of complementarity and synchronicity both attempt to explain the threads that interweave and connect the collective mental world with the physical world. Zeitgeist also applies between the development of these two theories: a bridge between similar concepts at virtually the same time in the absence of any collaboration.

While the science of physics may be difficult to understand, William Blake (a philosopher, artist, and poet who died in 1827) may have said it best. Blake wrote, "If the doors of perception were cleansed, everything would appear to man as it is, infinite..." (Keynes, William Blake, p154.) Incidentally, the rock group "The Doors" took their name from this Blake quote.

Zeitgeist between existential philosophy and the motorcycle began in nineteenth century Europe. As motorcycling evolved, individuals' involvement in riding tended to express existential themes. The existential themes we will be dealing with are freedom, meaning, personal responsibility, fear/anxiety, and death. These themes are outlined in the book, *Existential Psychotherapy* (Yalom, Irvin D., M.D., NY, NY: Basic Books: a division of Harper-Collins Publishers, 1980.) I have modified them in terms relevant to motorcyclists.

1. Freedom - The motorcycle has long been a cultural symbol for freedom. The individual who rides often experiences a feeling of freedom.

2. Meaning - If motorcycling is an important part of an individual's identity, then being a motorcyclist adds meaning to one's life.

3. Personal Responsibility - Motorcyclists must take personal responsibility for their own safety. It is up to the rider to make him or herself visible in traffic, to watch for road surface hazards, and so on. Many motorcyclists take pride in the sense of personal mastery it takes to ride a motorcycle.

4. Fear and Anxiety - Motorcyclists rarely talk about this among each other. However, most motorcyclists have at one time or another experienced a certain fear or anxiety about riding. Concerns such as, "Will I be safe today?" "Will I be injured?" or "Will I embarrass myself in a group ride?" are all common fear- and anxiety-based concerns about riding.

5. Death - Everyone is going to die. That's a given. However, most motorcyclists are more consciously aware of the possibility of death due to a motorcycling-related accident than are most car drivers (even though this is also a statistically high probability). Some studies suggest that a motorcyclist is 16 times more likely to die in an accident than if he or she were driving a car.

In 2002, there were 63,730 fatalities due to influenza in the USA. Additionally, thousands of people die each year due to accidents in their own homes. I mention this only to highlight the importance of keeping a balanced perspective. Don't get locked into the belief that you will die as a result of being a motorcyclist. Everyone dies, and one certainly doesn't need a bike to accomplish this inevitable event.

While there are other existential themes, the ones above are the ones most relevant to motorcyclists. From these five themes, undoubtedly the one that will ring immediately true is—FREEDOM. Suffice it to say that freedom is a subject that most motorcyclists have thought about in relation to riding. However, the existential themes of meaning, personal responsibility, fear/anxiety, and death are also relevant to motorcyclists, though they are not as readily or commonly acknowledged.

This is because existential themes are typically experienced as free-floating emotions rather than concrete ideas. (The distinction between these will be made clear in Chapter 6.) It has been my experience with post-accident motorcyclists that it is important to clarify these free-floating feelings. So doing helps to illuminate emotional ambiguities. Defining these issues aids in the goal of emotional healing after an accident.

While existentialism started out as a philosophy, it took root in the field of psychology around the turn of the twentieth century. It was at this time that existential themes were identified as individually and psychologically relevant. Before this was realized, critics believed that existentialism was a philosophy for revolutionaries, anarchists, and rebels. (This is interesting, because motorcyclists or "bikers" at least, have been given some of these titles at one time or another: (More zeitgeist!)

We now know that existential themes are psychologically significant for understanding the human condition. For motorcyclists, existential themes are psychologically active and immediate.

While the five existential themes with which we are concerned are relevant to most avid motorcyclists, the rider with PTSD tends to experience them in their more negative, conflicted form. Each of the five existential themes and their conflicted forms will be dealt with separately in the following chapters. For now, it is important that these themes have been identified by way of introduction to forthcoming chapters.

CHAPTER 4

Freedom

In 1998, the Guggenheim Museum in New York City presented its revolutionary exhibit, The Art of the Motorcycle. Ultan Guilfoyle, a Guggenheim staff member and curatorial adviser, commented that, "The myths of the twentieth century are very much the myths of the motorcycle—love, speed, sex, death, danger, and freedom" (*American Motorcyclist*, Oct '98 p. 24). Freedom! What true motorcyclist hasn't experienced a feeling of freedom and all the joy it brings to riding?

Motorcyclists are people who are uniquely aware of how freedom feels. They know the experience of freedom, not just the theory. The experiential world is different from the theoretical world. The motorcyclist is a person who has discovered how to capture his or her own joy and knows it. It is not uncommon for a motorcyclist to be riding solo on a twisty mountain road and to let out a spontaneous shout of joy, or to be riding on a beautiful day through incredible scenery and suddenly burst into song! At these moments, a motorcyclist knows it's good to be alive.

Alas—such sweet pleasures are only bestowed upon those who have a passion for something in life. However, just as logically, those who feel the greatest passion are also capable of feeling despair in equal measure.

Despair is a crucial emotion. It can act as a guidepost that points toward change. In *The Iliad*, Homer wrote,

"Strength is felt from hope and from despair." It is at the point of despair that one can begin to let go of problematic issues before they cement within. It is at the point of despair that there is no way to go but up. So great is the power of despair that Alcoholics Anonymous asserts that most individuals cannot give up drinking until he or she has "hit bottom." Despair can act as a catalyst to renew or develop personal strengths and assets.

For a motorcyclist with PTSD, despair can be truly cutting. Suddenly the lifeline to freedom and joy appears to be severed. His or her connection to freedom now comes into conflict, and a feeling of helplessness sets in. Now, and often against the individual's better judgment, freedom through riding becomes a questionable pursuit.

A key concept of existentialism is that people are innately endowed with an essential freedom and therefore have a large role in shaping their own destinies. On a conscious level, not everyone is aware of this individual freedom, because on the surface, life can sometimes seem to offer few choices. Nonetheless, from an existential perspective, in order to live an authentic life (that is, a life in which we as individuals assume responsibility for our own choices), we must utilize our individual freedom to choose among alternatives.

For a motorcyclist, suffering from PTSD seems to take away not only his or her capacity to experience freedom while riding but also the freedom to choose to ride. For now, the capacity to experience freedom while riding and the ability to choose to ride seem to be in hand-to-hand combat with seemingly uncontrollable fear and anxiety. In this way, PTSD can act as a veritable prison in which a motorcyclist's freedom has been captured. On a deep level, the individual now has a feeling of being trapped and confused, instead of being the free agent he or she once was.

Freedom for a motorcyclist has two distinct components:

1. Experiential freedom refers to the hands-on experience of riding.
2. Theoretical freedom refers to the idea of riding and the knowledge that one is a motorcyclist— the identity component. Theoretical freedom involves the freedom to choose to ride and the ability to dream of riding free from debilitating PTSD-related fears. It is no wonder that for a motorcyclist with PTSD, the loss of individual freedom to ride can be psychologically devastating.

The loss of freedom carries with it the implication of being enslaved by an entity that has taken away your freedom. For post-accident motorcyclists, the slave-master is PTSD. To emphasize the psychological intensity that the knowledge or feeling that you are enslaved brings, one need only remember that throughout history, people have been willing to die for freedom. Individuals such as Socrates (freedom of speech), Joan of Arc (political and religious freedom), and John Paul Jones ("Give me liberty, or give me death") are just a few examples of a lineage of people who have died in the name of freedom. A loss of any kind of freedom strikes a terrible discord with collective as well as individual humanity.

In *Beliefs, Attitudes and Values* by Milton Rokeach (San Francisco: Jossey-Bass, 1968), statistical studies found that freedom is ranked the highest value among the majority of people. In *Freedom and Civilization* (Malinowski, Bransilaw, New York, 1944, p. 74) Malinowski wrote, "Freedom is very much like health or virtue or innocence. We feel it most intensely after we have lost it."

To illustrate how the loss of freedom affects motorcyclists, one need only think of the continuing battle fought for the freedom of choice to wear a helmet. For motorcyclists, this fight is about experiential and theoretical freedom. The experiential component is obvious: some riders physically don't want to wear a helmet. The fight for theoretical freedom comes from the desire to be free from the mandates of bureaucrats. When bureaucrats dictate what a motorcyclist must do or not do, a master-slave dynamic is set up. This is the theoretical loss of freedom that includes a restriction on personal choice, thereby interfering with individual identity. From this, a sense of being enslaved is felt that many motorcyclists find unacceptable.

People are not comfortable without their freedom. Once it's lost, they will do almost anything to get it back. Individuals who live in free countries are particularly sensitive to the loss of freedom, because they have so much of it. For the individual motorcyclist then, the loss of experiential and theoretical freedom due to PTSD causes a great deal of internal conflict.

In order to help you on your quest to determine if you should ride again, it is helpful to identify and list the ways in which you believe your freedom has been taken from you due to your accident and PTSD. Take your free-floating emotions and transform them into concrete ideas. How do you feel? Make a list. Do you feel angry? If so, that's good. Explain the reasons for your anger, and use your anger in an appropriate way to facilitate change. Do you feel frightened? Write about what fears you have.

Examine your past relationship to fear and how it has changed due to your accident. To further this knowledge, decide how you would like to react to fear. Recall times in your life when you were pleased with the way you dealt with anger and fear. How can you apply those same characteristics now? Or think about people whom you admire and analyze how they dealt with anger and fear. Don't be hesitant to draw upon sources other than yourself as a guide for how you would like to be. It is a basic psychological principle that role modeling is a key force in shaping people's lives.

There are several fitting quotes on the topic of freedom with which I would like to sum up this chapter. The first comes from the book *Tao of the Ride* by Garri Garripoli (Deerfield Beach, FL: Health Communications, Inc., 1999, p. 79): "When you let go of everything you cling to for safety, you are free...When you shed the restraints that come from what other people expect of you, you are free...Isn't that one reason why people like to ride motorcycles? No restraints, no safety net, nothing to hold you back..."

In the book, *Ethics And Ambiguity* (Simone de Beauvoir, Secaucus, N.J.: Citadel Press, a division of Lyle Stuart, Inc., 1948, p. 70), the author wrote, "Freedom must project itself toward its own reality through a content whose value it establishes." (de Beauvoir was a French existentialist and John Paul Sartre's longtime woman friend.) For the avid rider, that chosen content and value is motorcycling.

By now, you have learned how to begin to make a self-directed choice about riding based upon the characteristics of your individual identity. This coupled with your thoughts on freedom can help you to strengthen your resolve about whether to ride again or not. You are now getting closer to making a choice based upon a clearer understanding of your motivations. Psychologically, it is better to make choices as an extension of your individual identity, not as an extension of your PTSD.

Back in the Saddle Again

CHAPTER 5

Meaning

The question of why some people become avid motorcyclists has often been asked. It has been said that a satisfactory answer has never been given. From a psychological perspective, and certainly from an existential one, the answer is simple: because it adds meaning to life and is an aspect of one's individual identity.

A uniquely human trait is the struggle for meaning. Most adults eventually reach a point in life when they ask questions such as, "What gives my life significance?" "What can I do to add meaning to my life?" These questions and similar ones are existential in nature.

Often a psychological crisis is brought on by dramatic or traumatic life events. For a motorcyclist, a riding accident may be such an event. This is known as an existential crisis. Suddenly, the significance of being a motorcyclist turns into a psychological/existential conflict as a result of PTSD. A major indicator of such an internal crisis is a marked feeling of ambivalence toward taking up riding again.

A basic tenet of existentialism is that an individual must actively do something in order to self-actualize, or as existentialists would say, to be an "authentic self." According to existential principles, an authentic self has ideals and convictions that are formed from within, not subject to outside influences. An "Inauthentic Self" holds ideals and convictions that are largely formed in reaction to the expectations of others, and therefore change in accordance with the social environment in which one finds oneself.

The existential themes and exercises in this book are designed to help you identify what makes up your authentic self. Once you have a clearer understanding of this, you are better equipped to make authentic choices. Each individual has both the freedom and responsibility to interpret and create a self-significant, authentic identity. Often, being a motorcyclist is an authentic identity component.

Be careful that you don't devalue the significance that motorcycling may add to your life. Since riding is generally thought of as a recreational activity, people can hold the belief that it is not very important, especially if one has PTSD. Non-riders can be particularly persuasive in convincing motorcyclists that riding is a nonessential component of life. However, if being a motorcyclist is a part of your identity, don't fall into the trap of believing that it is not important. Remember that being an authentic self means that you hold onto your own inner beliefs, which may not be the same as the beliefs of others. Freud said that people need three things in life: love, work, and play. Play is an important part of life. From play we learn about life and about ourselves. Recreation gives people a sense of rejuvenation. And even though this may be difficult for some people to understand, for many motorcyclists riding becomes more than play. Therefore, when a post-accident motorcyclist questions the value of riding, an identity or existential crisis may result.

The struggle for meaning in life is very much a part of our industrialized society. Industrialization made leisure time possible. From leisure comes a certain freedom, a freedom to choose among options. In some ways this complicates life, because we now have a greater personal responsibility to create individual identity and meaning. In pre-industrialized civilizations, people may have been less likely to experience an existential crisis of meaning, because in these civilizations, individual lives were filled with arduous tasks of daily living. Things that we take for granted today had to be created by hand; people had to make their own soap, paper, and clothing. Basic survival was paramount. Leisure time was scarce.

Moreover, in these civilizations, societal roles were designated to people instead of the result of a self-directed choice. Religion dominated their collective worldview while science dominates ours. Pre-industrialized people had a feeling of belonging to a larger unit without having to discover one for themselves. Their day-to-day survival responsibilities were great. Modern responsibilities are great, too, but in a more internal, individualized way. So an individual's passion for motorcycles can be seen as a struggle for meaning in the midst of leisure time.

Existentially, there are many roads to meaning in one's life. Two that are most common are hedonism and altruism. Hedonism is a life philosophy that was identified around the third and fourth centuries B.C. and was available only to the wealthy of that time.

Basically, hedonism is a philosophy that asserts that pleasure and happiness are the only things of true value. To illustrate how seriously we take this view today, just think of how pervasive the notion is that we are all somehow born with the God-given right to be happy. The right to pursue happiness is even in the American Constitution, as well as pervasive in the media. We are likely to change jobs simply because we are not happy; we end marriages and relationships because we are not happy. People of pre-industrialized societies didn't do this. Their priorities, ethics, and even their notion of happiness were different from ours today.

In modern times, hedonism has been translated into what we call the "pleasure principle." The modern hedonist view asserts that even seemingly selfless people such as the recently deceased Mother Theresa or Ghandi lived selflessly only because it brought them pleasure to do so. From the view of the pleasure principle, the guiding light which shines the way toward meaning for a motorcyclist is that riding brings one pure pleasure.

Be careful not to confuse hedonism with selfishness. In this chapter, hedonism for motorcyclists refers to the ability to experience pleasure, which is a good thing. Psychologically, if one is unable to experience pleasure, it may be a symptom of depression or a psychological blockage. Being able to feel pleasure is psychologically healthy. Herodotus, a philosopher who died in 425 B.C., said, "If a man insisted always on being serious, and never allowed himself a bit of fun and relaxation, he would go mad or become unstable without knowing it." Of course, in contemporary times, the word "man" includes women, too.

The second road toward meaning is altruism. Like hedonism, altruism as an ideal can be traced back to pre Judeo-Christian times. The altruistic view posits that meaning is found through giving and sharing with others. The Judeo-Christian religions embraced this idea. These religions teach that meaning can only be found through selflessness, and selflessness is not, according to this view, a product of the pleasure principle. Rather, it is a sort of relinquishing of the self in favor of more God-like attributes. Accordingly, only by infusing one's self with selfless attributes can an individual find true meaning in life.

To illustrate how motorcyclists as a group seek and demonstrate meaning through altruism, one need only recall all the charity rides for which motorcyclists are known. Today charity rides are given in almost epidemic proportions; they are given on holidays and on nonholidays, for charities and sick children. They are given to benefit diseases, poverty, injuries, and just about any cause imaginable.

Some say that altruism comes when hedonism fails. In other words, when one cannot be fulfilled by hedonism, one seeks meaning through altruism. Others say that hedonism and altruism are mutually exclusive. Still others believe that the two are overlapping and interrelated. From my professional experience with motorcyclists, I would say that the pursuit of motorcycling is the latter, both hedonistic and altruistic.

The degree to which you experience hedonism and/or altruism is more food for thought in your equation of life's meaning as derived from being a motorcyclist. By thinking about meaning in life, and how it is interwoven with hedonism and altruism, many a post-accident motorcyclist comes to realize just how important being a motorcyclist is for him or her. Thinking in these terms will further your understanding of how and why (or if) being a motorcyclist is truly important to you.

Back in the Saddle Again

CHAPTER 6

Personal Responsibility

Most would agree that motorcyclists are personally responsible for their own safety and for accepting the inherent risks of riding. Taking personal responsibility to navigate one's way through life is a lesson that a person can learn from the art of motorcycling. In this way, motorcycling is a metaphor for life.

According to existential psychology, people are responsible for directing their own lives. This is the way to become an authentic self, as described in the previous chapter. Being inauthentic, then, refers to not accepting the responsibility to discover your authentic self and to use its features to make self-directed choices. Living an inauthentic life means allowing others to choose your course for you and then perhaps blaming them for the choices made.

J.P. Sartre, a French existentialist who died in 1980, believed that guilt is a result of being inauthentic and refusing to commit to a personal choice. Sartre asserted that we are composed of the choices we make. Being inauthentic means allowing others to choose for us. Being authentic means identifying what is valuable to us and choosing accordingly. Choosing to ride again should be just as much of an authentic choice as choosing not to ride again. Either choice is fine, as long as it is authentic.

For some, motorcycling is not an important part of their identities. Often these people were urged to ride by husbands, wives, or friends who are avid motorcyclists. If this describes you and your choice to ride, now is the time to take personal responsibility for having allowed yourself to be persuaded. There is no one to blame if it was you who allowed yourself to be nudged into something that really didn't interest you in the first place. If this is the case, use this book to develop a new sense of personal identity and responsibility. Utilize the techniques and ideas given here to learn how to make authentic, self-directed choices. Practice, and get in the habit of saying "no" when confronted with an uncomfortable choice. With patience, you'll be surprised how easy it really is.

Often people who are easily persuaded to go along with others' ideas have a feeling that to say "no" is the same as hurting, disappointing, or offending others. This usually isn't really true. And if occasionally it is, it must be realized that others also have personal responsibility toward their own choices and feelings. If you have a history of being afraid to say "no," it is probably something that is rooted in childhood experiences. This is something to discuss with a professional.

It is futile to blame yourself for not having been able to say "no" in your past. Chances are you were doing what you thought was right at the time. Blaming the self or others never solves problems.

It is not uncommon for post-accident motorcyclists to be bombarded with concerns from others about riding. Loved ones are often frightened at the prospect of an injured motorcyclist choosing to ride again. This is understandable. Those close to you do not want to lose you. These loved ones can become very emotional when they learn you may take up riding again. It is important to be understanding about this. They are showing that they care about you. However, ultimately, the choice must be yours if you are to be an authentic and self-directed individual.

Many a post-accident rider finds him or herself not only dealing with personal aftereffects from the accident but also having to comfort concerned loved ones. This can be a great burden. It is important to remember that *you* need your energy now to recover. Expending too much energy on comforting others may only serve to slow this process down. Be kind and reassure the people close to you as best as you can, but take the personal responsibility to voice what you need from them. This includes making it clear to others what you can do in terms of comforting them and what you cannot. It includes speaking up for yourself and allowing others to know how they can support you.

You may find that letting others know how they can support you is actually comforting for them. Once they know exactly what they can and should do for you, they are likely to feel more in control and better able to handle their own emotions. Likewise, this approach is in line with accepting personal responsibility regarding the aspects of your recovery that are within your control.

It is also helpful to understand that some people, usually other motorcyclists, may be uncomfortable around you. Realize that this is because your accident may represent their own worst fear having been realized through your experience. Individuals who feel this way may try to avoid you or act nervous around you. Chances are that they feel guilty about this but can't seem to help it. One way to deal with this awkwardness is to let people know up front which subjects you are comfortable discussing. You may decide that you don't want to discuss the accident with people, but you're more than happy with other topics of discussion and their company. The choice is yours as to how you want to handle these people. Let them know what you choose. By doing so, they will feel more comfortable around you, and most importantly, you will feel more comfortable around them.

In order to identify clearly what you need now, and to further assist you in making your decision to ride again or not, below is a technique to try from a branch of psychology called cognitive/behavioral psychology. This technique involves identifying and separating **thoughts** from PTSD-related **feelings**. In clinical terms, the word "cognitive" refers to your thoughts. The behavioral component is the action stemming from your cognitive thoughts.

Cognitive/Behavioral psychology also deals with feelings. This branch of psychology encourages people to identify feelings, think about feelings, and finally to separate feelings from cognitions. This is because feelings are not cognitions. Cognitions are thoughts. Feelings are often accompanied by physical counterparts, whereas cognitions are only thoughts. For example, with PTSD, the feeling of fear is often hand-in-hand with a pounding heart, shaking, sweating, etc. Let's look at another feeling and the physical counterparts that accompany it: happiness. The behavioral aspects of happiness are smiling, laughing, perhaps jumping for joy, etc.

Thoughts, on the other hand, are less likely to bring up dramatic physical counterparts. Moreover, a feeling can be described in one word. A thought takes at least a sentence. Here are some examples of feeling words:

afraid	bitter	glad
alone	resentful	whole
angry	anxious	needy
appreciated	depressed	kind
calm	content	proud
caring	elated	able
competent	fulfilled	silly
guilty	peaceful	powerful

Feel free to add to this feeling list as you see appropriate. See if you can identify the behavioral components to each of the feelings on the above list. What would your physical reactions be?

Since cognitions take at least a sentence to express, an example of cognition could be, "Motorcycle dealerships can vary on the sticker prices of their bikes," or "I am late." Now, the feeling component behind this thought may be disappointment, anger, or indifference. But the thought is just a thought with no judgment. With practice, one can learn to identify the feeling and separate it from the thought.

Use this technique to aid in your psychological recovery. Do this by identifying and separating PTSD-related feelings and symptoms from your authentic self. Learn the difference between symptomatic PTSD feelings and authentic self-characteristics so that you do not mix up the two. PTSD symptoms are not the authentic you. They are simply very good at tricking you into believing that they are due to their intensity.

Moreover, keep the cognitive/behavioral technique in mind if you begin to ride again. Identify PTSD symptoms as feelings and separate them from your thoughts while motorcycling. When you recognize PTSD feelings, including their physical counterparts, (i.e. fear, shaking, queasiness), shift your focus to the appropriate thoughts (e.g., "This road is similar to where I had my accident, BUT it IS a different road"). You may need to do this as much as 10 times a minute at first. Be patient and practice. Eventually it will become natural.

Appropriate cognitions while riding include thinking about your riding environment, scanning your environment, and thinking about the proper riding skills. Clearly, your thoughts serve as a much better guide to your actions than PTSD-related feelings.

Imagine yourself riding with PTSD emotions and think about what types of riding behaviors may result. Clearly, your riding behaviors may suffer significantly. Now imagine yourself riding with a focus on thoughts that include proper riding skills and how this would influence your riding behaviors. Do you see a big difference here? Focusing on your thoughts tends to make you feel calm and clear-headed. Appropriate, synchronistic behaviors will follow.

On some level, many motorcyclists tend to have an innate understanding of personal responsibility. The act of riding is one that demands a sense of individual mastery. If you've had an accident, think of ways you can transfer the sense of mastery that you once felt into your recovery now. To do this, it is helpful to remember times in your life when you have made decisions based on authentic self-directions. From these memories, draw conclusions about what traits you possess that can help you to be authentic and masterful now. Try making a list of your appropriate skills.

Finally, it is your personal responsibility to make sure that you develop a good social support network to assist with your psychological recovery. Make an effort to connect with others who have been in accidents. Contact some local riding groups and ask around for anyone with whom you may connect. Or seek a good therapist whom you can trust.

Humans are social animals. Even shy people or loners are still socially interconnected with others to some degree. Psychological recovery is expedited by openly sharing your feelings and experiences with others. In fact, isolating yourself from sources of social support is a sure way to exacerbate any feelings of depression that you may be experiencing.

Asserting your personal responsibility in any situation takes courage, but it does become natural with practice. In the words of Amelia Earhart, "Courage is the price that life exacts for granting peace."

CHAPTER 7

Fear and Anxiety

Fear and anxiety have been placed in the same chapter instead of separate chapters, because these emotions are interconnected. On an emotional spectrum, if one feels fear, one also experiences anxiety. Likewise, if one feels anxiety, fear is just around the corner. This chapter begins with the emotion of fear.

For people in industrialized countries such as America, fear seems to be a significant mental health concern. As a group, we appear to fear just about everything. Insistent reminders constantly bombard us with the notion that life is to be feared: wear a safety belt, wear a helmet, don't go out at night, learn self-defense, be wary of strangers, don't travel alone, don't eat fat, stay away from caffeine, and so on. We also fear not measuring up to others, and we definitely fear change. The list goes on ad nauseam.

This is not to say that there isn't some truth to all these concerns. But if absolute safety (which is an illusion anyway) is to be our main goal, then what of adventure? What of fighting for a cause? What of seeking personal truth? What of searching for meaning? In short, a life ruled by fear is a life unlived.

A common issue that comes up in therapy is the fear many clients have regarding their core identities. Many people have a deep-seated fear that their true selfhood is something bad or wrong, that no one would like them if this inner self were revealed. Clinically, this is usually due to old childhood messages that repeatedly play in an individual's head. It's not the person's fault; it is simply what they have learned. But what is learned can be unlearned. In a book called *Feel The Fear And Do It Anyway* (Jeffers, Susan, PhD., NY, NY: Ballantine Books, 1987, p. 4), the author writes, "...fear may look like a psychological problem, in most cases it isn't. I believe it is primarily an educational problem..."

Many fears are free-floating and can intrude into one's mind, seemingly out of the blue. The sudden intrusiveness of fear is a clue that it is coming from the subconscious. In clinical terms, this is called "internalization."

See if you can identify old fear-based messages that may have come from your childhood. To assist you with this exercise, use the cognitive/behavioral technique you learned in the chapter on personal responsibility. Make a list of your free-floating fears both before and after your accident. Recognize where they may have come from and counteract them with your logical, cognitive, authentic side.

Recognize that free-floating fears, while they may masquerade as thoughts, are actually feelings—fear-based feelings. Practice challenging these feelings by using your thoughts to rationalize and even to "parent" these feelings. Sometimes is it helpful to think of the character Spock from the TV show *Star Trek*. One need not be a fan of the show to use Spock as a sort of role model for separating fears from your authentic self.

Once you have identified a free-floating fear, ask yourself what Spock would have to say about it. Spock would dissect this fear by weighing it against logic and evidence. Like anything else in life, the more you practice this technique, the easier it will become. Remember, often it is your thoughts (your "Spock" side) that can guide you better than your feelings, particularly if PTSD is an issue. Moreover, if you decide to get "back in the saddle again," use your Spock side to calm your fears while riding. With practice, this will prove to be very helpful.

Although rarely acknowledged, it is not uncommon for motorcyclists to have free-floating fears concerning riding. Some of these fears are social fears, such as, "Will other riders think I'm no good?" "Will I be able to ride as well as others in my riding group?" "Will I embarrass myself?" Other common fears for riders are based around injury or even death: "Will I be killed today?" "Will I have an accident?" When you think about it, it is not strange that motorcyclists should have free-floating, injury-based fears.

In America, most of us grew up with the message that motorcycles are deadly. At the end of almost every motorcycle movie ever produced, the rider dies. At one point in our motorcycling history, a term was coined— "murdercycle." This awful term was coined in the early part of the twentieth century after a traumatic racing accident on the old board tracks of the time.

Even though many motorcyclists live as long as the rest of the population, those who become injured or killed stamp a deep impression on our collective consciousness by reaffirming the old myths. An event which is negative or catastrophic is what psychologists call "salient." Salient happenings are compelling to humans. Catastrophic events often become salient, overshadowing good events. Again, think of Spock to counter any salient, catastrophic feelings.

However, for the post-accident motorcyclist, an accident may be a fear now realized. One client said to me, "I'm kind of glad the accident happened. Now the mystery is gone. Now I know it is possible to survive accidents and go on to ride again." Another client reasoned that one of the deciding factors in his decision to ride again was "a strong desire to overcome fear."

But others may not be so fortunate in their attitudes. Sometimes this is because their accident caused a permanent physical challenge. If this is you, it is important that you grieve your loss. It is normal to go through emotional stages of grief and loss as presented by Kubler-Ross (discussed in detail in Chapter 11). These stages are represented by the acronym, DABDA: Denial, Anger, Bargaining, Depression, and Acceptance. Generally speaking, it takes about two years to adapt to a permanent physical challenge.

Allow yourself to go through these stages and then ask yourself: are you a victim or a survivor? If you are a victim, you may forever live in fear, thereby thwarting your potential to recover to the best of your ability. If you are a survivor, you will eventually take personal responsibility for your recovery.

While the term "accident victim" has been used in this book, it was used by way of shaking you up a bit and perhaps causing you to realize that the word "victim" didn't sit well. Now it is time to validate this and think in terms of being a survivor. The key to being a survivor is to focus on small goals, always refraining from the next goal until you are comfortable with the previous one. Survivors don't focus on the results as much as the tiny goals to reach success. Results are realized only through actualizing tiny goals first.

According to Jeffers (p. 28), "Pushing through fear is less frightening than living with the underlying fear that comes from a feeling of helplessness." Since a sense of helplessness is often a symptom of PTSD, a post-accident motorcyclist may not only feel afraid of motorcycles but also begin to fear his or her own choices to make *any* sound decisions.

To counter this feeling of helplessness, take an inventory of your life and decide in which areas you can take control. Look at your relationships with others, as written about earlier. Also, think of ways you can take personal responsibility toward your physical recovery. While it is normal to fear the physical change that may have happened to you, reframe your fears and think of them as internal signs that you must move forward, not backward.

If you have become permanently physically challenged, educate yourself about how you can deal with these challenges. Get social support from others who are similarly injured. Physically challenged people have many opportunities today. There are motorcyclists who were paralyzed from the waist down who decided to ride again. So, too, are there riders who lost a limb and chose to ride again. Recall the case example of the attorney Bradford in this book. He and others have had their bikes customized to meet their physical challenges, and they do just fine.

Individuals from many different kinds of sports have been injured, not just motorcyclists. Some skiers who were permanently disabled ski on mono-skies. Of course, it is not necessary that you follow suit. But it is important that you take the responsibility to educate yourself and learn about your possibilities and strengths, despite your limitations. After all, who in life doesn't have some kind of limitations?

ANXIETY

Now we come to anxiety—the flip side of fear. Like so many emotions, anxiety has physical counterparts. Typical physical symptoms of anxiety can include sweating, shallow breathing, and trembling. In existential philosophy, anxiety is thought of as a natural condition of living. However, existential psychology breaks anxiety down into two categories.

The first category is normal anxiety. Normal anxiety is a response to being faced with a choice. This type of anxiety can be used as a catalyst toward change. Typically, normal anxiety is experienced as a growing awareness that it is up to the individual to dare to take a step toward self-directed change. Normal anxiety involves an awareness that no one else can make a decision for you, and that it is up to the individual to "face the music" dependent on his or her choice. Of course, it is also up to the individual to take the personal responsibility to educate him or herself, seek professionals and friends who can offer support about making a choice, but in the end, there will come a time when the individual realizes that the ultimate decision is his or hers. At this time (and even before, as awareness grows) a feeling of existential angst (intense anxiety) is normal. If identified, clarified, and handled by the authentic self, this angst can actually be empowering. The personal empowerment comes from the knowledge that this anxiety is an internal message that it is time to choose your unique path. And that this time of choice is an opportunity to actualize your authentic character through action.

Neurotic anxiety is the second type of existential angst. This is anxiety in its conflicted, negative form. This type of angst seems to emotionally paralyze a person. In Samuel Beckett's 1952 play, *Waiting For Godot*, the play ends with these lines:

Vladimir: Shall we go?

Estragon: Let's go. *(Stage direction: No one moves.)*

Everyone has some kind of neurotic anxiety. The degree to which the anxiety immobilizes a person is the measuring stick that indicates the level of neurosis. Just as anxiety is a normal tenet of the human condition, so, too, is ambiguity. From an existential perspective, we must learn to live with, tolerate, and convert anxiety and ambiguity into signals that we need to make a self-directed, authentic life choice. It is unreasonable to think of eliminating any and all anxiety and ambiguity as a goal for our lives. If we were able to do this, we would cease to be human. Anxiety is normal. How one handles it is key.

For a post-accident motorcyclist, choosing to ride again or not isn't the only choice to be made. How to deal with family and friends as a result of your choice is just as important for your sense of integrity, as well as for your resolve. If you are continually angry, upset, and annoyed with the questions, comments, and opinions of others (and there will be many), it may indicate that you are in a neurotic angst—that you have not made a decision as to how to deal with others concerning your choices.

Realize that your decision could change over time and that it is normal to experience anxiety and ambiguity despite having once made a choice. However, eventually there will come a time when acting upon a choice will become paramount in order to avoid becoming stuck in neurotic anxiety. Having made a decision and having taken steps toward acting upon that decision indicates that your level of anxiety is normal. Neurotic anxiety, as you recall, is immobilizing and so prevents active choices, just as in the ending of Beckett's play.

Some useful guidelines to assist you in making choices as to how to deal with others at this time include a basic understanding of what psychologists call "Boundaries." Neurotic existential angst includes a lack of understanding of where you as an individual ends, and where another person begins. This indicates a lack of personal boundaries and often causes a kind of merger between someone else's feelings and thoughts with your own. This is called Internalization.

Internalizing the attitudes of others is seen by existentialists as a clue that an individual is being inauthentic. If this is you, it is useless to blame yourself for this. It is simply something you learned. In some cases, a person's childhood didn't allow for developing a sense of personal boundaries. As an exercise, try to identify ways in which you may not have had the opportunity to learn personal boundaries growing up. Write these down and analyze them, or bring them up with a therapist.

Use the cognitive/behavioral techniques in the chapter on personal responsibility to learn how you really feel and what you really think as opposed to what others feel and think. Additionally, below are some useful guidelines for identifying whether or not your boundaries are intact. The first list details boundaries of an authentic self:

1. Your boundaries are intact if you relate to others only with whom mutual respect is possible.

2. Your boundaries are intact if you interact with others out of mutual agreement or compromise.

3. Your boundaries are intact if you can say "no" when you mean "no."

4. Your boundaries are intact if you try to be aware of personal choices.

5. Your boundaries are intact if you can keep your mental and physical privacy.

Some signs that indicate that your boundaries are not intact and that you may be behaving in an inauthentic way include the following:

1. A pattern of trying to create intimacy with, and gaining approval from, people who are not respectful of you.

2. A pattern of believing that others are somehow better than you are.

3. A pattern of saying "yes" when you really want to say "no," along with a pattern of agreeing with others when you really don't. Or not being able to identify how or what you actually feel and think and therefore simply adapting to the ways of others.

4. A pattern of allowing others to choose for you.

5. A pattern of allowing others to intrude upon your mental and physical space.

If you see yourself as needing to improve upon your sense of personal boundaries, use the above guidelines to monitor your behavior. When you identify yourself acting in ways that are inauthentic, practice changing these ways of interacting. It's best to begin with the least anxiety-producing interactions. As long as you are motivated and commit to practicing setting up your boundaries, you'll do just fine. Naturally, you'll experience some anxiety around this, especially at first. But remember, anxiety is neurotic only if it immobilizes you.

Back in the Saddle Again

CHAPTER 8

Existentialism and Death

This chapter has been titled "Existentialism and Death" for two reasons: (1) death is a key topic for existentialism, and (2) it is better to buffer the chapter title in order to minimize any reader's anxiety by having the big, bold word "DEATH" looming over this page. While the concept of death (or non-being, as many existentialists call it) causes some angst in almost everyone, death will remain an omnipresent topic and must be confronted.

The ending of one's life is the ultimate form of death, but during life there are many small deaths: divorce, loss, permanent injuries caused by an accident, completing school, and retiring all represent tiny deaths in one's life. Psychologically, from the standpoint of individual evolution, these small deaths are, in their way, a sort of blessing. After all, if not for tiny deaths throughout life, how could one eventually come to terms with his or her own physical demise?

For the existentialist, death actually gives meaning to life. In the book, *Existential Psychotherapy* (Yalom, 1980) the author explains that life and death are interrelated. Even though physical death destroys our bodies, the idea of death can save our lives.

The concept of death gives significance to life. It is because we will die that it is all the more important to find meaning in life and to develop an authentic self. De Beauvoir, in her book, *Ethics And Ambiguity* (p. 34) wrote, "...it is because there are real dangers, real failures, and real earthly damnation that words like victory, wisdom, or joy have meaning." This is why, for many motorcyclists, deciding to continue to ride or not is an important life question. After all, being a motorcyclist can be a very meaningful life component for some people. Motorcycles can add meaning to one's life by being a part of a person's authentic identity.

Severe death anxiety, which causes a person to become immobilized (also a symptom of PTSD in the form of avoidance behaviors), is thought of as an indication that an individual may not be living an authentic life. This person may be living a life in which he or she allows others to make decisions for him or her. So deep down, intense fear of death is actually a fear of life—it is a fear of dying without having truly lived.

After deciding to ride again after an accident, one client said to me, "I figure if I die on my bike, at least I'll die doing something I love. I'll die being the real me, which, I guess, is better than dying doing something I don't care about, like being in a rush hour accident trapped with my colleagues in the office car-pool van."

It is essential to think about death if we are to think about life in a significant way. Indeed, if we are to establish an authentic identity and find meaning in life, we must give thought to death, not in a preoccupied or morbid way, but in a life-affirming, self-actualizing way. In the book *Existential Psychology* by Rollo May, Ph.D., (Upper Saddle River, NJ: Prentice-Hall, 1961, p. 65), May wrote, "The price for denying death is unidentified anxiety, self-alienation."

What May refers to as "unidentified anxiety" is what is referred to in this book as "free-floating" anxiety. As mentioned in the chapter on Fear and Anxiety, motorcyclists, like the rest of the population, are not immune to free-floating anxiety. Free-floating death anxiety may be the root of all fears and anxieties. A client of mine once said, "I think maybe motorcyclists are the nicest people around 'cause they all secretly have free-floating fears that they're going to die any minute."

Perhaps my client had a good point. However, there is more to it than that. Psychologically, the term "Ecstasy of Unity" refers to the primal sense of belonging one experiences when in the presence of one's own tribe. For many riders, this ecstasy of unity is a significant part of being a motorcyclist and so contributes to the general friendliness of riders toward one another.

Free-floating death anxiety can be quelled by living an authentic life. Further, utilizing the cognitive/ behavioral techniques you've already learned is helpful. Logically weigh free-floating, anxiety-based feelings against the logic of your thoughts. Remember, it is very possible to live a long life and still be a motorcyclist; the two are not mutually exclusive—in spite of Hollywood movies that seem to find it poetic to have motorcyclists die at the end of films.

The fear of death is a primal one and does not appear to be unique to humans. The idea of conceptualizing one's own inevitable demise may be unique, but all mammals will attempt to flee if faced with the possibility of imminent death.

For humans, death anxiety seems to be composed of a number of smaller anxieties. In a study by Diggory, Rothman, Doreen ("Values Destroyed by Death," *Journal of Abnormal and Social Psychology*, Vol. 63; No 1, 1961, pp. 205-210) the authors questioned a large sample of people and concluded that common death fears are ranked accordingly:

1. My death would cause grief to my relatives and friends.

2. All my plans and projects would end.

3. The process of dying might be painful.

4. I could no longer have any experiences.

5. I would no longer be able to care for my dependents.

6. I am afraid of what might happen to me if there is an afterlife.

7. I am afraid of what might happen to my body after death.

Existentially, all of these fears about death seem to lead to one thing: a fear of losing one's self, a fear of nonbeing. The antidote to this? Yalom, in *Existential Psychotherapy*, (p. 45) asserts that, "If we can transform a fear of nothing to a fear of something, we can mount some self-protective campaign...or plan a systematic campaign to detoxify it." In other words, if we can transform our fear of nonbeing into a fear of being inauthentic, thereby giving us a strong desire to be authentic, then we can begin to live our lives to the fullest. If we are living our lives to the fullest, we have transcended the fear of death to the best of our mortal capacity.

CHAPTER 9

Rider's Intuition

Mike had been a diehard biker for some 20 years. Throughout those years he had owned a succession of custom choppers of his own design and making. I could tell from my first meeting with Mike that here was a guy whose identity included being a biker.

Mike hobbled into my office on crutches, wearing a cast on his left foot. On his right foot, he wore a black leather boot. His leather vest had "Harley Davidson" written on the back. Mike had come to me seeking counseling to help him to overcome the debilitating anxiety he was experiencing over the thought of riding again after his accident. Although Mike's accident had happened only two weeks prior to my meeting with him, it was important to Mike that he learn how to handle his anxiety now. He wanted to get back on his bike as soon as the cast was scheduled to come off.

During my initial intake session with Mike, one of the first things he said to me was, "The day of my accident, I woke up with a bad feeling. I wish I had listened to my gut. I feel strange admitting it, but I think I somehow knew I shouldn't ride that day."

Intuition—many motorcyclists have experienced it. Some will reluctantly admit to it. Others choose to label it as "gut instinct" or some other phrase that they believe carries less of a superstitious connotation.

For our purposes, I have chosen to call it "Rider's Intuition" (R.I.). While R.I. may seem like a self-explanatory phrase, some qualification is necessary. First, I have chosen the word "rider" to indicate specifically motorcyclists who will be actively engaged in the act of riding. I am not talking about a motorcyclist's ability to intuit something like the stock market.

Secondly, I have chosen the word "intuition" due to its definition in terms of accuracy for our cause. Webster's Dictionary defines intuition as, "immediate apprehension or cognition." The Latin root of the word "intuition," which can be found in a Latin/English dictionary, means "to guard and protect."

Understand that I am speaking about a psychological occurrence. I am not talking about Extra Sensory Perception (ESP), mysticism, or spirituality. (Individuals who have spiritual beliefs are certainly welcome to apply them as they see fit.) With this in mind, the key questions for motorcyclists are as follows: *Does rider's intuition really exist, and if so, how can a motorcyclist harness it as part of a plan to minimize future riding risks?*

The answer to the first question is Yes. It is possible that R.I. can and does exist. While it would be an error to think that R.I. is an exact science, it is also an error to think that intuition cannot exist. This is because the mind often has a funny way of perceiving subtle environmental, physical, and emotional cues. In order to understand this from a psychological perspective, it is necessary to understand something about the subconscious mind.

The subconscious is the part of the mind that houses information of which the conscious mind may not be fully aware. At times, and under certain circumstances, the conscious mind may not be equipped or motivated to deal with certain information. So this information is stored in the subconscious. However, the subconscious is still a part of our psychological makeup. It is not a separate entity and so cannot simply fall into the ethos and leave the conscious mind alone.

Instead, the subconscious communicates its information in ways that might not be easily recognizable. One of these mysterious modes of communication can be intuition. In Edgar Mitchell's 1996 book, *The Way Of The Explorer* (Itasca, IL: Putnam Publishing Group, 1996, p. 15), Mitchell, a former Navy pilot who became an Apollo missions astronaut and later founded the Institute of Noetic Sciences, (which, in part, studies quantum physics) wrote, "Life in the military can mean relying on that vague faculty of intuition on a regular, if not daily, basis." When writing about his experiences landing airplanes on small aircraft carriers, Mitchell wrote (p. 5), "It was intuition you depended on...what I lacked in my early years was an understanding of how intuition, emotion, and intellect all interrelate."

Dr. Gary Schwartz and Dr. Linda Russek, who wrote the book *The Living Energy Universe* (Charlottesville, VA: Hampton Roads Publishing,1999), refer to the work of the late Dr. Jonas Salk who thought that when reason and intuition join hands toward a common goal, the result is greater than the sum of its parts. For example, when oxygen and hydrogen mix, they create a water molecule: the two joined become a whole that is greater than the two separated. So there is scientific evidence that substantiates the validity of intuition when understood and accepted by reason.

Therefore, if a rider like Mike believes he had an intuition not to ride on a certain day, it very well could have been that it was Mike's subconscious mind attempting to alert him about some subtle environmental, physical, or emotional cue. Subtle environmental cues could be anything from traffic patterns to ensuing weather conditions. For example, let's say that Mike's intuition came from a subtle environmental cue. In this case, Mike's intuition may have been a communication from his subconscious mind warning him that his riding skills weren't perfected in ways to deal with the day's weather elements. This information, being too hurtful to Mike's pride, may not have been readily available to his conscious mind and so would be stored in his subconscious. This information may have left Mike with a vague feeling that something was off that day.

Or let's say that Mike's intuition came from a physical cue. In this case, it may have been that Mike had recently taken a medication that was still affecting his reflex responses. This effect may have been so subtle that Mike didn't consciously consider it as a relevant factor. However, his subconscious was on the alert and so initiated a communication in the form of an intuition.

On the other hand, let's say that Mike was experiencing emotional stresses that he tried simply to forget. While Mike may have thought that forgetting his current troubles was possible, his subconscious may have communicated to him a warning that his ability to concentrate was diminished.

As you can see, there are a myriad of psychological reasons as to why information may be stored subconsciously and then communicated as an intuition. Due to these psychological conditions, it is reasonable to assert that R.I. can exist.

With the knowledge that R.I. can exist, let's move on to our next question: *How can a motorcyclist harness R.I. as part of a plan to minimize future riding risks?* While it is true that much of R.I. is a subjective experience, there are several steps you can take toward harnessing it. Learn to distinguish R.I. from PTSD symptoms as well as from typical, pre-accident free-floating anxieties and make a commitment to trust it. R.I. cannot work for you if you do not trust it.

In order to distinguish R.I. from PTSD symptoms or free-floating anxieties, you must compare the difference between PTSD-related symptoms and free-floating anxieties routinely experienced, to the experience of an intuition. Can you recall a time in your life when you had a "gut feeling" to do or not do something, and it turned out to be right? Quantum physics validates these experiences as an occurrence called "feedback loops." As applied to psychology, feedback loops are thoughts, emotions, and behaviors that are interrelated.

Feedback loop theory comes from a branch of quantum physics called "systems theory" (Schwartz and Russek, 1999). Interestingly, psychology has its own systems theory, which asserts essentially the same principles. Systems theory in both quantum physics and psychology asserts that all systems are interconnected as opposed to reductionistic, meaning existing in an unconnected or isolated way.

PTSD symptoms are often experienced as physical realities. Autonomic functions such as a pounding heart, shallow breathing, and sweating result from PTSD symptoms. This differs from free-floating anxieties, which are worries that an individual may routinely have, such as a persistent fear/anxiety that your bike will get a flat or run out of gas. For motorcyclists, these "free-floats" typically existed before an accident but may intensify after an accident.

Intuition, on the other hand, is usually not experienced in dramatic physical terms and is not a free-float that typically plagues you.

Therefore, the first thing to decipher when determining whether you are experiencing R.I. is to notice the absence or presence of exaggerated, physical

PTSD responses, as well the absence or presence of recurring free-floats. If you have no exaggerated autonomic responses and your feeling is not a typical free-floating anxiety, it may be time to consider the possibility that you are experiencing R.I.

The next step in harnessing your R.I. involves making a commitment to it. This step includes trust. Remember Mike's statement: "I should have listened to my gut"? Listening to one's "gut" is not as easy as it may sound. There are many reasons why a rider may choose to ignore R.I. (Naturally, you will ignore it if you don't trust it.) To prove the point, imagine this scenario: You have been planning a weeklong vacation on your motorcycle. For weeks now, all of your free time has been going into planning this trip. To complicate matters, you will be taking this trip with a friend. The day of your vacation you awake with what you think may be a R.I. and say, "Oh, no! What should I do?" Obviously, the easiest thing to do is to convince yourself that you cannot trust your intuition. However, what if you decide that you do trust it? Do you cancel the trip? Don't worry; such a drastic step is not usually necessary. However, you may want to postpone the trip until the next day.

This is because R.I. is rooted in psychology, not mysticism or ESP. Therefore, it can only inform you on a particular day about that same day. Chances are that you have not suddenly become a clairvoyant who can predict what will come a week from now. Instead, R.I. usually foretells possibilities that could affect your riding safety on the actual day of your intuition.

R.I. may not always be cautioning you to something as drastic as avoiding an accident. It could end up being something merely inconvenient, such as a mechanical problem or running into a storm. The following is a case example of such an R.I.:

Bonnie, a 32-year-old motorcyclist, awoke one morning with what she thought was a gut feeling not to ride that day. However, the weather was sunny and beautiful, and so Bonnie convinced herself that this gut feeling was probably nonsense. In any case, it was certainly too inconvenient to worry about. So Bonnie went ahead with her solo plans for a day trip to the mountains. By the time Bonnie had almost reached her destination, she began to feel dizzy and nauseous. In fact, she became so ill while riding that her vision began to blur. Pulling over to the nearest rest stop, Bonnie felt faint as she dismounted her bike. Her nausea became so bad that she was forced to call a friend to come and get her and her bike in a pickup truck. Several days later, Bonnie discovered that she was pregnant.

It appears that Bonnie's R.I. was a message from her subconscious warning her about her unknown physical condition. So while Bonnie was fortunate enough not to have had an accident, she would have been better off had she trusted her R.I. on that day.

Committing to R.I. is an important step toward harnessing it. If you commit to R.I., you are more likely to experience it, because your psychological defense mechanisms are less apt to reject the intuition when it is received. You will be less likely to resort to defense mechanisms such as denial or rationalization. Denying that you are experiencing R.I. or rationalizing yourself out of it are ways that you could trick yourself out of listening to your "gut feeling." In order to avoid these mental tricks, you need to make a sincere commitment to R.I.

Further, it is a good idea to make a commitment to R.I. with a trusted riding friend. In this way, you will have an outside source of support that can help you to stick to your commitment.

One word of caution is advised: Since R.I. is not an exact science, much of your experience with it will be subjective. It is certainly possible that you could go for months, even years, without experiencing R.I. After all, many motorcyclists ride for years, or even a lifetime, without having an accident. Nevertheless, if you are going to incorporate R.I. into your safety management plan, it is best to trust and commit yourself to it at all times.

This is the only chapter with which I urge the reader to use caution. This is because there is no empirical evidence of which I am aware that has specifically and measurably tested R.I. Though R.I. can be supported by quantum physical and psychological evidence of feedback loops, all actual evidence of R.I. in this chapter is anecdotal. The development of the concept of R.I. came largely from the files of my own clients, as well as research into the discoveries and theories of systems theory from quantum physics and psychology.

All other chapters in this book are supported by either empirical data or established theories. If the concept of R.I. is too overwhelming for you at this time, simply don't use it. Rely upon your own judgment as to whether or not R.I. is something you wish to explore now, in the future, or not at all.

For more information on Rider's Intuition, check out an article I wrote for *Motorcycle Consumer News* (*MCN*), titled "Rider's Intuition," December 1999. For back issues of *MCN* and reprints of "Rider's Intuition," as well as other articles authored by me and published by *MCN*, contact Ian Smith Information: (303) 777-2385.

CHAPTER 10

Self-fulfilling Prophecies and Waking Hypnosis

In the field of psychology, the term "self-fulfilling prophecy" refers to a mental process that is largely subconscious. Self-fulfilling prophecies occur when an individual has a belief in something, and by virtue of that belief, puts into motion events that will make that belief happen. While the person may or may not be consciously aware of the belief in question, subconsciously he or she takes steps that will produce a result that is fitting with the belief system.

Here is an example that I experienced with a group self-fulfilling prophecy:

About 10 years ago, there was a terrible abduction and murder of a little girl in an area not far from my home in California. After the poor child's body was found by police, a rumor began to spread all over town and beyond that on a certain blank billboard near the freeway where the girl's body was discovered could be seen a ghostly image of the child's face at sunset each night.

The news media quickly capitalized on this rumor due to the large number of people who were gathering by the roadside to see this image. I decided to go and see for myself what was happening.

As I arrived at the location, hundreds of people were already there gazing at the billboard. I, too, looked at the billboard. What I saw was light and shadow from traffic and the setting sun. As I walked around in an attempt to see the board from different angles, I overheard what people were saying to one another. Strangers were talking to strangers who would then send the word on down the line to umpteen other strangers.

I was tapped on the shoulder by a young man about 20 years old. His eyes were fixed on the billboard, his jaw slightly agape, and he said, "It's amazing! Do you see her?" I said, "No, can you point her out?" The young man pointed, making a circular motion with his finger as if outlining a face. Then he said "...and there is her mouth and her eyes." Still, all I saw was light and shadow from the traffic and setting sun. However, as I walked around some more, I did begin to notice that from a certain angle a dim shadowy outline of a large tree from across the street could be detected.

This is an example of a group of people seeing what they believed was there—a group self-fulfilling prophecy. Now, one could argue that it was I who experienced a self-fulfilling prophecy, that it was I who believed that nothing was there and so saw nothing. Still, the point has been made about how powerful a self-fulfilling prophecy can be.

Given the power of self-fulfilling prophecies, imagine the potential impact an old biker saying such as, "There are two kinds of bikers: Those who have been down and those who are going down" could have on a person. This old adage gives the impression that crashing is a sort of rite of passage. (This adage also does not qualify what "going down" means.) Thus, the ambiguity of the phrase tends to conjure images of doom and gloom. It's important to watch for catastrophic cognitions and realize that "going down" doesn't have to mean a tragic accident. It could refer to a simple parking lot spill that, incidentally, doesn't even require a motorcycle. Many people have taken spills in parking lots simply by tripping over their own two feet or slipping on a banana peel.

So any rider who buys into this old saying in a catastrophic way may increase his or her chances for trouble due to the psychological principles of self-fulfilling prophecies. Further, it can benefit you to know that prestige has an impact on the power of suggestion. If the person who suggests the inevitability of a crash sometime in your biking career is a long-time rider or holds some sort of riding prestige in your eyes, you may be more prone to accept and believe in what he or she tells you. The influence that the statement has on you may be in equal proportion to the authority or prestige you give the person. What must be realized here is that even those who are respected in our eyes do not hold the cards of fate for another individual.

This is certainly not to suggest that a rider can't or won't go down if he or she changes a belief system. It is to suggest that it's psychologically sound to be careful what you buy into. Your mind is everything. It's because of your mind that you ride in the first place. The focus here is on psychologically increasing or decreasing potentials. There are many riders who have never been in accidents. There are also motorcyclists who have been in one or two crashes and never have one again. Anything is possible. Don't allow others to convince you that you will be in an accident sooner or later. Just because someone else has experienced motorcycling in a certain way doesn't mean your experience will be the same. Remember your personal boundaries and authentic self. Be clear about where you end and another person begins.

WAKING HYPNOSIS

Hypnotic theory has a similar concept to self-fulfilling prophecy called "waking hypnosis." A famous hypnotist, Dave Elman, who taught medical doctors how to hypnotize patients, wrote a seminal book called, *Hypnotherapy* (Cross Plains, WI: Westwood Publishing Company,1964, p. 67) in which he states, " A waking suggestion is a suggestion given in a normal state of consciousness..." Elman went on to write, "For example, someone in a room yawns. Someone sees him yawn, and he yawns, too. Another person sees him yawn, and the third person yawns, and pretty soon you have a room full of yawning people." This is the power of waking hypnosis. In fact, simply reading the above quote may make you yawn!

An example of waking hypnosis may be experienced by you right now, at this very moment. To demonstrate this, read carefully the next statement in quotation marks. Be sure to follow all directions:

"Right now, at this very minute, scan your body for an itch. Within sixty seconds that itch will absolutely need to be scratched. You feel an itch coming on now...you know that you have a terrible itch beginning to surface. You know it, you feel it. You've been feeling it coming on for a while. Now, scan your body for that itch. Itchy, itchy, itch." Now reread the statement again; then stop reading for sixty seconds, close your eyes, and scan for that itch.

Chances are that about 80 percent of readers did indeed find an itch or will in a few moments. As you can see, waking hypnosis is very similar to self-fulfilling prophecy, the only real difference being that waking hypnotic suggestions don't necessarily rely upon an underlying belief system. Waking suggestions can occur immediately and without your knowledge or belief.

Elman gives an important example in *Hypnotherapy*, p. 73: "An accident patient is rushed to the hospital. He seems to be in bad shape. He's in a mixture of shock and panic. In the emergency room he hears the reassuring words, 'not serious; he'll make it; he'll do all right.' Those magic words 'not serious' have probably saved thousands of lives."

If your accident has resulted in the necessity of surgery, here's a great and easy hypnotic technique you can use to enhance your recovery. Write down on a piece of paper the best possible outcome of your surgical procedure. Be sure to state it in terms of what you DO want, NOT what you DON'T want. There should be no "don'ts" or "nots" in your statement, only positives. The word "pain" should not be in your statement.

An inappropriate statement would be something like this: "I will not feel pain." Since the subconscious has a funny way of blocking out negative words such as "not," it may only hear the word "pain." Therefore, it is best to state what you do want in the positive. For example, "I will feel comfortable" would be an appropriate hypnotic statement. After you have jotted down an appropriate statement, give it to your doctor or recovery room nurse. Usually they are more than willing to oblige you by reading your statement in your ear just as you go under the anesthesia or just before you awake from the operation. Since you will be unconscious, your conscious mind will be bypassed, and a direct route to your subconscious will be available for the suggestion. This is a powerful hypnotic tool. However, because you will be unconscious, it cannot correctly be called waking hypnosis. This could simply be termed "unconscious hypnosis."

Likewise, when you ride a motorcycle, it is not psychologically sound to say to yourself, "I don't want to hit that obstacle." Framed in this negative way, the subconscious will likely persuade your eyes to fixate on the obstacle, thus increasing your chances of hitting it. (Recall the saying, "Look at your obstacle; hit your obstacle.") Instead, say to yourself, "I want to ride through my exit or my escape route." Practice this as much as possible. You'll be surprised how powerful such thoughts are.

To give you an example, some years ago before I became a hypnotist, I was riding my dirt bike through some pretty hairy trails. Ahead of me to the left, I could see a huge pile of rocks surrounding a boulder. I could also see that there was a clear trail to the right, which, naturally, is where I wanted to go. As I approached the point where I could change my direction, I kept saying to myself, "Don't hit that obstacle...Don't hit that boulder." Well, inevitably I did indeed hit the boulder, despite the fact that I knew where my exit route was. My mind had fixated on the word "obstacle." Fortunately, I was wearing full protective gear and was unharmed.

Always remember, there is nothing as powerful as the power of suggestion.

CHAPTER 11

Post-accident Stages of Emotional Recovery

Psychological recovery after an accident comes in stages. A variety of recovery stages exists as theorized by different mental health professionals. For our purposes, I have chosen two models of emotional recovery. The first is Dr. Elizabeth Kubler-Ross' five stages of recovery from her 1973 seminal work, a book titled *On Death and Dying* (NY, NY: Collier, 1970).

While Dr. Kubler-Ross originally identified these stages for individuals who are dying, these stages are also relevant for accident survivors and their loved ones. In fact, the Ross stages are used for any type of loss in life such as divorce and loss of job.

The second emotional recovery model is from the work of Barry Richards, LCSW in his 1989 book, *Thriving After Surviving* (Pleasant Grove, UT.: RoseHaven Publishers). The reader will find similarities between these two models of recovery. Usually, individual recovery ping-pongs somewhere in between the two theories. Further, although each model is presented in separate stages, in reality the stages are experienced as overlapping and fluid. As you familiarize yourself with these stages, be sure to keep in mind all that you have learned about PTSD as well as all the other psychological material presented in this book. It is likely that PTSD symptoms and other issues you have learned about in *Back in the Saddle Again* will be intertwined throughout the stages of emotional recovery.

Emotional recovery after a motorcycle accident is affected by many psychological factors. The stages presented in this book are meant to serve as a guide as to what individuals may typically expect. However, pre-accident coping skills, stress tolerance, support systems, pre-existing psychiatric diagnosis, and developmental factors are all elements which will affect the degree to which an individual will experience emotional trauma after an accident. Therefore, it is important that individuals consult a mental health professional in order to gain a clear understanding of personal emotional recovery.

The Kubler-Ross five stages of emotional recovery as relevant for post-accident motorcyclists are summarized as follows:

(1) Denial - This is the initial stage where the survivor often feels the need to protect him or herself from the overwhelming awareness of what has happened. During this stage, survivors tend to soften the psychological impact of what has happened to them. Frequently the survivor will repeat such phrases as, "I can't believe this has happened to me."

(2) Anger - This is the stage where survivors ask, "Why did this happen to me?" During this stage, it is not uncommon for survivors to feel resentment toward others who have remained healthy and unharmed. For persons who hold religious beliefs, it is typical for them to feel anger toward God.

(3)   Bargaining -   At this point in the emotional recovery process, survivors—religious or not—begin a bargaining process with God or some power other than the self. Individuals may promise something of the self in exchange for what they have lost. Common phrases heard in this stage include, "If only I had," or "I promise I will…if I recover."

(4)   Depression - During this stage, the awareness of what has happened is now in full consciousness. The survivor admits what has happened and often becomes despondent. At this time, survivors may even reject visitations from friends and loved ones.

(5)   Acceptance - This final stage of emotional recovery is when survivors come to terms with their loss. This can be a time of personal victory during which the individual can marshal personal resources and prepare to move forward.

The second emotional recovery model by Barry Richards, LCSW, is summarized as follows:

(1)   The Survival Honeymoon Stage - During this initial stage, survivors typically feel an inner determination to regain what they have lost. Survivors tend to be grateful that their lives were spared and are anxious to return to their pre-accident lifestyles.

(2)   Adjustment Shock - This is the stage where survivors begin to doubt their ability to cope with the challenges that lie ahead. This stage may last anywhere from several weeks to years if professional help is not sought. During this stage, survivors sometimes feel abandoned by God.

According to Richards, individuals may experience four other reactions during this time:

a) Grieving - While grieving is a natural response to injury, survivors at this stage may feel grief akin to what is felt upon the death of a loved one.

b) Selective Hearing - Selective hearing protects an individual from processing news that may be too overwhelming to cope with at this time. Survivors may avoid hearing information that is painful. Instead, survivors may focus on information that brings them comfort.

c) Disequilibrium - A feeling of disequilibrium is natural for survivors of serious injury. Disequilibrium may be experienced as a sense that the body and mind are out of tune with each other. Survivors may feel frustrated that their recovery is not happening faster.

d) Anniversary Reaction - This can be a frightening experience, especially because it typically occurs during a period of successful recovery. Sometimes, anywhere from 11 to 13 months after the accident, survivors may experience traumatic memories around the time of the anniversary of the accident. It is not uncommon for post-accident riders to remember the exact date and time of the accident.

(3) Recovery - This final stage represents the successful adjustment to whatever losses have been incurred. The survivor feels encouraged instead of hopeless and focuses on personal strengths and abilities.

Realizing that emotional recovery comes in stages can act as a catalyst toward successful recovery. Further, it is important that you share your concerns with others. Communicating your concerns will help you to synthesize your thoughts and feelings. Doing so will aid in your individual emotional recovery.

Now that you have become familiar with these two models of emotional recovery, it is a good idea to review them again in order to identify where you presently fit on the continuum. Also, try to determine how your PTSD symptoms and existential issues fit into this picture.

While you can expect to go through stages of psychological recovery, it is really the PTSD that is preventing you from enjoying your motorcycle, provided, of course, that debilitating, permanent physical injury is not an issue. In the next chapter you will learn how to manage your PTSD symptoms. Once done, you will be well on your way to getting "back in the saddle again."

Back in the Saddle Again

CHAPTER 12

How to Overcome Fear of Riding

In Chapter One, you learned that PTSD is the reason you have been experiencing fear and anxiety over riding your motorcycle again. Since fear and anxiety are experienced in both emotional and physical terms, the techniques you will learn in this chapter are skills that will help you to manage these two-pronged symptoms. By so doing, you will be able to control and finally overcome your PTSD-related riding fears.

As you read this chapter, it is important to remember that change happens systematically. While you may want change to occur immediately, the reality is that successful change is a process that exercises itself on a progressive continuum. It is normal to feel that sometimes you take two steps forward and one step back. Eventually, this will subside as you come closer to psychological recovery.

It is natural for people with PTSD to question their ability to change. For those who suffer from PTSD, catastrophic thinking can be seen as part of PTSD symptoms. The steps suggested in this chapter will help you focus on your goals instead of your risks. After all, life itself is a risk; total safety is an illusion. True psychological risk involves giving up your freedom and responsibility to make self-directed choices toward change.

It is part of the human condition to experience what is known as the "Approach/Avoidance conflict." Whether you suffer from PTSD or not, all of us experience some moments of fear when we find ourselves approaching our goal.

When this happens, we may recoil and avoid the very thing we seek. For those who recognize that this is a natural first reaction, the key becomes to refocus on our goal and proceed again. While doing so, it is helpful to remind yourself that you have the right to gain control over your life. After all, you are here, you are alive, and you have a right and a responsibility to make authentic, self-directed choices, not only in regards to motorcycling but also to life in general. Ultimately, you alone have both the freedom and responsibility to allow yourself to work toward systematic change.

The techniques in this chapter are a combination of psychological cognitive/behavioral methods as well as hypnotic modes of recovery. These techniques are widely used in various combinations in the mental health field.

These techniques include (1) proper breathing, (2) progressive relaxation, (3) rating, (4) self-hypnosis, and (5) gradual exposure (sometimes called systematic desensitization).

Many elements of the cognitive/behavioral techniques outlined in this chapter originated from the early 1950's Russian space program experiments. These techniques turned out to be so successful in dealing with the anxiety of astronauts in training that the Russians later applied them to their Olympic athletes.

When, in 1976, the Russians won more Olympic gold medals than athletes from any other country, these techniques spread to other parts of the world. Soon after, these techniques were adapted by mental health professionals and used to treat Vietnam veterans with combat fatigue (now known as PTSD) as well as utilized for professional athletes in America and other parts of the world.

It is interesting to note that prior to the Soviets' experiments with these techniques, many physiologists believed that autonomic functions such as heart rate, bodily temperature, startle response, and muscle tension were beyond the control of the individual. What the Russians discovered was that certain methods could indeed be taught to individuals to manage these autonomic responses. Further, it was discovered that autonomic functions could be controlled without the aid of expensive laboratory equipment such as biofeedback instruments.

While the Soviets deserve much credit for our current understanding of the autonomic functions, a man named Jacobson should not be forgotten, though he is given little attention in psychological literature. In as early as 1938, Edmund Jacobson utilized relaxation techniques to help patients manage autonomic responses. References to Jacobson's practices are found in *Modern Hypnosis, Theory and Practice* (Ansari, Masud, Ph.D., Washington, D.C.: Mas-Press, 1982). Eventually, behavioral psychologists applied relaxation skills to their patients to help reduce anxiety. However, it wasn't until after the Soviet Olympic triumph in the 1970s that other countries applied these methods to what we now know as sports psychology.

First, it is important that sufferers of PTSD learn general relaxation skills in order to temper the symptoms of PTSD. Remember, PTSD-related feelings have physical counterparts. General relaxation skills are proper breathing and progressive relaxation. These skills should be learned before moving on to the more specific symptom abatement techniques which are rating, self-hypnosis, and gradual exposure.

BREATHING

Breathing is a basic autonomic function that is affected by our emotions. During times of tension, breathing becomes shallow, reducing the amount of air needed to nurture the brain and muscles. Under extreme stress, such as an anxiety reaction symptomatic of PTSD, the heart rate increases, making breathing irregular. The mind interprets this irregular breathing and rapidly pounding heart as a signal that danger is present. The body responds to the mind's signal of stress in like fashion, making the breathing even more irregular as the heart races even faster. Soon, a circular dynamic is established between the mind and body. At this point, the "flight or fight" response sets in.

The consequences of such a mind/body dynamic can be dramatic. Mental concentration is undermined. Physical coordination becomes impaired. Soon, fatigue sets in. It is at this point that some individuals may actually pass out. In order to counteract this circular mind/body event, you must first become aware of what is happening to you.

Becoming aware of your irregular and shallow breathing is the first step toward reversing this stress-related physical and emotional event. To counter this response, you must take steps to correct your breathing. Correcting irregular breathing has a surprisingly calming affect on the emotional intensity of the situation. This is because it is physiologically impossible to experience anxiety when the body is relaxed. The two states are incompatible. If you can cause your body to relax, stress reduces dramatically.

Causing your body to relax begins with proper diaphragmatic breathing. When an individual breathes properly from the diaphragm, the "flight or fight" autonomic responses begin to subside. When you breathe properly, your heart rate will begin to decelerate. Once your body and mind receive this message, anxiety abatement begins. Mental concentration is returned to normal. Physical coordination is improved.

It is interesting to note that while in the "flight or fight" mode, the blood rushes to the extremities and away from the brain. This makes the individual physically strong, but mentally the person loses a few good IQ points. The physical strength that comes from this blood rush to the extremities is, in part, the reason why even a tiny person can lift a car if his or her child is trapped inside. We have all heard of these stories.

The first step toward becoming a diaphragmatic breather is to discover how you usually breathe. Many people in industrialized societies are thoracic breathers. This type of breathing is located in the chest and does not allow the lungs to be adequately filled. Thoracic breathing is associated with the left-brain, which rules our logical thinking processes. When an individual breathes properly from the diaphragm, the "flight or fight" autonomic responses begin to subside. The combination of deep breathing and a calmer heart rate signals the mind and body that it need no longer assume the "flight or fight" posture.

In order to breathe correctly, you must focus on breathing from your abdominal area. This is diaphragmatic instead of thoracic breathing. Breathing from the diaphragm increases oxygen flow and stimulates a synchronistic relationship between the brain hemispheres. Here's how to begin:

Lie comfortably on your back and place your hand just under your rib cage. This is the highest area of your abdomen. Take a few deep breaths and notice how much or how little your hand moves. If your hand moves only slightly, not at all, or moves down, then you are a thoracic breather. If you are uncertain of your results, place your hand on your chest. Now take a few deep breaths. If you are breathing from your thorax, your hand will be noticeably moving up and down with each inhale and exhale.

To correct thoracic breathing, remain in a comfortable reclined position. Once again, place your hand on your abdomen just below your ribcage. Now take several deep breaths through your nose. In your mind's eye, make a visual image of your lungs. Focus on expanding your stomach as you inhale. You should feel your hand rise as you push out your stomach. When you exhale, do so through your mouth. Now repeat the process. As you do this, notice the movement of your hand. If you are breathing from your diaphragm, you will notice your hand moving up as your stomach expands with each inhale. Likewise, you will notice that your hand moves down and in with your stomach upon each exhale.

To double check if you are doing this correctly, once again place your hand on you thorax (chest) as you inhale and exhale. You will know that you are breathing correctly if you notice less movement now from your hand on your thorax than from when you first attempted this exercise.

Practice this technique daily. Take no more than five deep breaths at a time, rest a little, and begin again. Two or three one-minute sessions per day should be enough to teach yourself how to become a diaphragmatic breather. Also, during the day and evening you should periodically check and correct your breathing by simply placing your hand on your abdomen and noticing its movement.

Remember, your stomach should expand as you breathe in, not your chest and /or shoulders.

With practice, you will soon become a diaphragmatic breather. You will begin to notice that you feel calmer throughout the day. You will also notice that the time it takes for you to recover from physical activity will improve significantly. It is in your best interest to remember that during times of stress, feelings of anxiety and fear are your personal cues to immediately become aware of your breathing and correct it. As you move through the following steps, it is vital that you maintain proper diaphragmatic breathing.

Once you are "back in the saddle again" (if this is your goal), practice deep breathing as you ride. This will not only keep anxiety down but will also keep your brain alert and your body energized. The brain simply cannot function properly without enough oxygen. You will also find that on long days in the saddle, proper breathing will cut your recovery period in half. This is also helpful for dirt-riders who need a lot of energy, especially if they are in a competition.

PROGRESSIVE RELAXATION

The basic relaxation technique that you will be learning is widely used by many healthcare facilities. It is used by people with high blood pressure, cardiac patients, pregnant women, and people with anxiety disorders, including PTSD, as well as by those with a variety of other conditions. In the beginning of this chapter, you learned that there is no question that people can be taught to control their anxiety.

However, you must take personal responsibility and commit to relaxation techniques.

To begin progressive relaxation, make sure that you will not be disturbed for the duration of this exercise. There should be no noise to distract you. The lighting should be dim. Now, lie down in a comfortable position. Practice your diaphragmatic breathing taking five deep breaths.

Next, focus your attention on your feet. Create a visual image of those tired feet in your mind's eye. Notice and analyze how the muscles in your feet feel. Now, tense your feet by constricting the muscles as hard as you can. Hold for the count of three. Then relax your feet by releasing the muscle constriction.

Repeat this process again beginning with a mental image of your feet. Tense the muscles tightly. Hold for the count of three. Release. After having tensed and relaxed your feet twice, take a moment and notice how much more relaxed your feet are now as compared to when you began this exercise. Feel the difference? Good. If you're not sure, do the exercise one or two more times. Soon you will notice a difference. After having relaxed your feet, take five more diaphragmatic breaths.

The rest of this progressive relaxation exercise will be exactly the same, but your focus of attention will move up to different sections of your body. Use the same tense and relax technique as you move up your body in sections. For example, your calves will be the next section, then your thighs, buttocks, back, shoulders, and neck until you reach your head and face. You will become progressively more and more relaxed as you relax each section of your body.

At times you may notice that particular muscle sections need more than two times of tensing and releasing. This is because most of us tend to carry tension in particular areas of the body. By focusing on your body in sections, soon you will learn where you tend to hold most of your tension. The shoulders and neck are common physical locations where people carry tension. Your areas of tension may vary. Once you have located these areas, you will find that you can quickly relax yourself throughout the day simply by tensing and releasing these areas only, along with your proper diaphragmatic breathing.

Since it is not always possible to take the time to lie down and go through the entire progressive relaxation process, simplifying it to your personal tension zones will help you to adapt this technique to any circumstance.

One or two 20-minute sessions per day should be enough to train yourself to be proficient in this exercise. In approximately one to four weeks, you will find that you have become a real pro at relaxing yourself. Soon you will find that you can gradually reduce practice sessions. Of course, as with all of the techniques, you will get back what you put into it by equal measure.

Remember, the more you practice, the more adept you will become at relaxing yourself. As stated earlier, it is physiologically impossible to experience stress, anxiety, or fear when your body is relaxed. When you think about it, this is really quite an amazing realization.

After about a week or two of regular daily practice sessions, you will begin to feel more peaceful in your daily life. This is a wonderful feeling, but don't let it stop there. As with proper diaphragmatic breathing, let times of stress be your personal signal to utilize this technique. Now that you have learned how to relax yourself, you are ready to move ahead to a technique called rating.

Some of the following techniques, while widely used by mental health professionals with clients, have been, in part, adapted from the book, *Free From Fears: New Help for Anxiety, Panic, and Agoraphobia* (Seagrave, Ann and Covington, NY, NY: Faison Pocket Books, 1987).

RATING

Rating is a process that helps you to break down your fear of motorcycling into specific, trauma-related avoidance behaviors. A rate list details your fears of motorcycling by beginning with those fear-related behaviors that cause the LEAST amount of fear and avoidance and ends with behaviors that cause the MOST amounts of fear and avoidance. When you feel you have successfully taught yourself to breathe from your diaphragm and are feeling reasonably confident in your ability to use your relaxation skills, you are ready to do your rate list. This list is an important part of the systematic process of getting "back in the saddle again."

Generally speaking, most people will need approximately one to two weeks of practicing diaphragmatic breathing and the progressive relaxation before feeling confident enough in their ability to relax in order to begin a rate list. Some individuals find that they are able to make a rate list relatively quickly, simply by mentally recalling situations they have been avoiding. Others find that they need a week or more to make a list that accurately identifies these situations. A general rule of thumb is to work on your list for about 10 minutes a day until you feel confident of its completion. It is always possible to add to or change the order of your list at any time.

As an example, the following is how one client experienced his LEAST anxiety—producing avoidance behavior. "After my accident, I covered up all my bikes with a tarp. I didn't even want to look at them."

Here's how to begin your personal rate list. On a piece of paper write down as many situations and thoughts about motorcycles and riding as you can think of that you have been avoiding. As you begin to think of these situations, recall what you were doing and what behaviors you demonstrated when you experienced feelings of fear in each situation. (The mere anticipation of fear is one reason you are avoiding the situation.) This is why it is important to learn relaxation skills before doing your rate list. Since fear causes the body to go into the "flight or fight" mode, controlling your autonomic responses by using your relaxation techniques will allow you to approach each situation with much less fear.

It is necessary that you rate the situations you have been avoiding in order from least to most so that you will be able to work through them in a step-by-step fashion.

Once you have identified your fearful circumstances and jotted them down, briefly describe yourself in terms of what you actually do when you exhibit avoidance behaviors. For instance, for the client quoted previously, avoidance behaviors began with covering his bikes with a tarp. Covering the bikes was the avoidance behavior. Further, whenever he went into the garage, he would deliberately look away from his bikes. Looking away is also an avoidance behavior. These are examples of what he actually did to evade his fears and anxieties.

Let's look at how a different post-accident motorcyclist named Paul rated his avoidance behaviors:

1. Walking into the garage where I keep my bikes.

2. Walking over to the area in my garage where my helmet and riding gear are located.

3. Putting on my riding gear and helmet.

4. Sitting on my bikes.

5. Inserting the bike key into the ignition.

6. Turning the key and starting the engine.

7. Shifting the bike into gear.

8. Riding down my driveway.

9. Riding down the block.

10. Approaching the freeway.

11. Riding on the freeway.

12. Riding long distances.

13. Riding past the place where the accident occurred.

As you can see from Paul's list, the situation that he was most fearful of and avoided was number 13. Number 1 was a situation in which Paul felt the least degree of fear/anxiety.

By making this list, Paul was able to separate his fears and understand them in terms of PTSD-related avoidance behaviors. This helped him to understand that his fears were not as generalized and unmanageable as he had thought. After rating his fears, Paul was able to see that he was not as helpless as he had been feeling. Paul could now see that his fears could be systematically broken down into a solvable equation. As you shall see later, a rate list will be used in conjunction with self-hypnosis and gradual exposure. Keep your rate list in a special notebook for now. You will need it as we progress.

After completing his rate list, Paul had a better understanding that his fears were actually composed of a systematic, hierarchal design. This gave Paul the confidence that he could learn to control his fears by tackling them one at a time. And he was right. Within three months of his accident, Paul was "back in the saddle again."

So far, you have learned that your feelings of fear, helplessness, and hopelessness can be managed by breaking each down into specific behaviors. As you move on to the next step, it is important that you continue to practice your diaphragmatic breathing and progressive relaxation skills.

SELF HYPNOSIS

The next step to overcoming your PTSD and fears is self-hypnosis. Hypnosis is a form of mental rehearsal that creates neurological patterns in the brain. These patterns are then called upon when you perform a task in reality. Since the subconscious mind does not know the difference between real and imagined experiences, hypnosis is a powerful tool for overcoming fears, enhancing performance, and correcting behavioral and emotional problems.

Like the relaxation technique and diaphragmatic breathing, hypnosis is widely used in sports psychology programs. Many professional athletes use hypnosis to enhance athletic performance. Likewise, hypnosis is taught to people to control certain medical conditions. There are even dentists who use hypnosis rather than Novocain on patients.

Some mental health practitioners teach simple visualization skills instead of hypnosis. Generally, visualization is a technique that involves closing one's eyes and visualizing the desired results of a situation...and that's about it—pretty easy to practice, right?

Some professionals assert that visualization and hypnosis are the same. Others say the two are similar. Still others think that the two are different. I maintain that, while similar, visualization and hypnosis are different, with hypnosis being the better tool for change. After all, no one gets his or her teeth drilled by using simple visualization techniques. Hypnosis is more powerful than visualization.

In 1955, the British Medical Association accepted hypnosis as a viable treatment. In 1958, the American Medical Association also accepted hypnosis as a valid treatment. I have never heard that either of these associations officially approved simple visualization. Many medical doctors are certified hypnotists. In some cases, hypnosis is actually used in place of medical anesthesia.

Hypnotic techniques are designed to bypass the conscious mind and get right into the subconscious, thereby effecting change. Hypnosis employs techniques that are not used with visualization. For example, some hypnotic techniques that may be used include, but are not limited to, autosuggestion and distraction.

Even police departments sometimes employ the services of a hypnotist so that officers can remember important things, such as the license plate number of a vehicle.

The human brain produces four different brain waves that we know of:

(1) Beta - Waves that your brain gives off during your normal waking state.

(2) Alpha - Waves induced when daydreaming and under hypnosis. Interestingly, Alpha waves have also been detected in athletes while engaged in a sport.

(3) Theta - Waves present during the dream state of sleep.

(4) Delta - Waves detected during deep, reparative sleep.

While there are many myths about hypnosis, in reality hypnosis is perfectly safe. At no time will you be unconscious during hypnosis. Rather, hypnosis feels like a relaxed state of daydreaming. If an emergency situation arises while you are practicing self-hypnosis, you will be able to get up, be alert, and respond accordingly.

Images of half-conscious people performing tasks that are against their will while under hypnosis are pure Hollywood/Las Vegas fiction. Don't be fooled by stage hypnotists. Stage hypnosis is a specific skill that relies upon many social factors. Generally, stage hypnotists choose only those people in the audience who exhibit personality traits that will allow for an entertaining show.

The basic difference between self-hypnosis and hypnosis done by a hypnotist is that with self-hypnosis you are the one giving yourself the instructions for deep relaxation, imagery, and autosuggestion. Autosuggestion is simply internal dialogue that affirms the positive results you want. As you have learned in the section on waking hypnosis, be careful not to give yourself suggestions that have the word "don't" or "not" in them. Remember, your suggestions should be stated in terms of what you DO want, not what you DON'T want.

Six basic elements can help you to get the most powerful effects from self-hypnosis. The first is to establish a single goal along with a suggestion to repeat to yourself about accomplishing that goal. For our purposes, your goals are singled out on your rate list, from the least anxiety-producing behavior to the most anxiety-producing behavior.

With this information in mind, it's time to return to your rate list. Begin with your least anxiety-producing situation on the list. Now, lie down in a comfortable position and begin with diaphragmatic breathing. Next, begin progressive relaxation. Then, imagine that you are some place relaxing and safe, such as a beach or in the woods. Now, make the scene real by bringing in all your senses. Imagine the sights, sounds, smells, tactile sensations, and tastes (if possible) of your relaxing setting. Lastly, focus your attention on something pleasant and soothing in your scene, such as the sound of the ocean or the sight of a tree in bloom.

As you imagine yourself in this relaxing setting, focusing all of your senses on one component, slowly allow yourself to shift your focus to mentally rehearse successfully moving through your first-rated fear, feeling calm and in control—your anxieties are physically placed in this peaceful environment. Approach the first one. Once again, bring in all of your senses to make the imagery real. As you do this, repeat your autosuggestion to yourself. If you find that, in your mind, you begin to sabotage the success of your least anxiety-producing scene, simply go back to concentrating on the one focal element in your imagined environment—a tree or ocean waves lapping at the shore, for instance. Take five deep breaths and then allow yourself once again to imagine your first-rated scene through to its successful completion. As you do so, remember to repeat your autosuggestion silently to yourself (e.g., "I am approaching my favorite bike in the forest/ocean/ desert"). If you find that your mind wanders, don't worry—simply refocus. If you still experience anxiety— perhaps try changing your imaginary setting. Imagine you are approaching the bike in a museum or seeing magazine photos of your bike.

Continue in this fashion until you have successfully imagined yourself completing your first-rated fear. You may need three to seven days or more until you are successful in imagining your way through your first anxiety. Continue in this manner with each of your rated fears in the hierarchy. Try to practice this at least once a day for 10 to 20 minutes—more if you have time.

If you are uncertain whether or not you are hypnotizing yourself, try a few "convincing" techniques. Just before you imagine yourself moving through your rated anxiety, suggest to yourself that your eyes are growing very heavy and will not open due to deep relaxation. Then, try to open your eyes, imagining that you are so very relaxed that your eyes simply will not open. Imagine that this is actually happening, and make it so. If you have trouble with this, just pretend it is happening and make it so..."Act as if." Another technique to convince yourself of your hypnotic state is to suggest to yourself that your hand is beginning to tingle, as if falling asleep. Suggest to yourself that you will lift your hand one time, drop it, and you will then feel the slight tingle sensation. Again, if you have trouble with this, just pretend it is so.

You will need to develop a new suggestion to repeat to yourself that matches the desired goal for each rated anxiety. However, before you move to the second-rated anxiety, it's time to learn the last technique toward overcoming your fears, a technique called gradual exposure.

GRADUAL EXPOSURE

Gradual exposure is the last technique for you to learn to overcome your fears and anxieties. Like the other techniques in this chapter, gradual exposure is a widely used psychological, cognitive/behavioral technique. Just as the term implies, it is key to expose yourself gradually to your fears in order to systematically overcome them. Do not attempt to manage more than one fear or anxiety at a time. As stated earlier in this chapter, be careful not to move to the next fear on your rate list until you have self-hypnotized and successfully, physically, gradually exposed yourself to each previously-rated fear/anxiety-producing situation.

After you are successful with hypnotizing yourself through your first anxiety (that is, you are able to imagine yourself moving through the first rated fear without sabotaging it), then actually, physically carry out the rated activity. Be sure to repeat your autosuggestion to yourself at least three times (more if needed) before and during your actual physical performance of the activity.

If, for example, your first fear is like Paul's, you will now walk into the garage just as you have been self-hypnotizing yourself through this situation. At the same time, you will be saying your autosuggestion silently to yourself. Walk into the garage breathing deeply, relaxing the areas of tension in your body, repeating your suggestion and walk out. This is all you need to do!

Learning theory teaches us that it is best to learn in sets of threes. So in Paul's example, he walked in and out of the garage three times and then stopped for the day. He continued to work in series of threes on a daily basis until he was ready to move on to his second-rated avoidance behavior. For Paul, becoming confident with his first fear took only two days. Your results may vary, and you may find that you need more or fewer self-hypnosis sessions and gradual exposures with each rated fear. This is normal individualism. So if necessary, utilize gradual exposure in a more frequent manner by performing sets of three, two or more times a day. Self-hypnosis for each rated fear is always followed by gradual exposure to the same rated fear before moving to the next anxiety on your rate list.

Do not move to your next rated fear/anxiety until you feel that you are so comfortable with the one before it that it has actually become boring! Believe it or not, this will happen, provided you have followed all instructions and repeated them as necessary. If you find that you still have a high-anxiety state during gradual exposure to your rated fear, simply go back to the self-hypnosis for a few days. Also, reevaluate your autosuggestion to make sure it is stated in positive terms. Additionally, you may want to reevaluate your first-rated fear. Perhaps you can now identify that you have a different first-rated anxiety than what you originally thought. If this is so, you will need to re-rank your rate list.

Now, go through your proper breathing, progressive relaxation, and self-hypnosis and attempt once again to gradually, physically expose yourself to the anxiety-producing situation in a set of three consecutive tries. Soon you will find that you are calm when physically facing your first fear. In fact, it will soon cease to be a fear. As soon as you feel comfortable with performing your first-rated task, it's time to move on to number two on your rate list and conquer it in like fashion. Continue in this way until you reach your last goal—the final rated anxiety.

Be sure that you don't push yourself beyond the rated goal that you are working on. Even if you feel that you can handle it, don't! For example, Paul's eighth-rated goal was to ride down his driveway, calmly. After having successfully hypnotized himself around this goal, he then performed three sets of physically riding down the driveway. And that's all Paul continued to do for three days until it became boring. He knew it was time to move onto his next fear because after utilizing the gradual exposure technique, not only did he begin to feel bored, but he also felt confident and peaceful around this rated activity.

Though tempted, Paul was careful not to allow this feeling of peacefulness to push him beyond his listed ratings. He knew he must proceed in a step-by-step fashion in order to successfully reach his ultimate goal of getting "back in the saddle again." One can think of this in mathematical terms: If you recall high school algebra, you'll remember that one can't skip a step and expect to end up with the correct answer.

It's okay to back step along the way of each goal if needed. For instance, if you have reached your fifth-rated goal and suddenly find that all your anxieties come flooding back (this is called relapse), simply go back to square one, your first-rated fear. You will soon find yourself right back on track.

You now know all the steps toward successfully getting "back in the saddle again." None of the steps is particularly difficult; they just require practice and patience.

Moreover, you have learned a great deal about your individual identity and how you can make self-directed, authentic choices. You have learned about PTSD and personal boundaries. You have learned a lot about fear and anxiety. You have learned about the stages of emotional recovery, and more. These concepts and techniques can also be used to manage and overcome just about anything in life.

Lastly, it is my hope that you have gained a new understanding of just how important being a motorcyclist can be. In closing, I'll leave you with these sage words from Martin Luther King Jr.:

"The ultimate measure of a person is not where they stand in moments of comfort and convenience, but where they stand at times of challenge and controversy."

With the knowledge you now have, whatever authentic, self-directed choice you make, things can only get better.

Bonus Chapters for Motorcycle Clubs

CHAPTER 13

Motorcycle Clubs

How to Use Psychological Techniques to Increase Group Cohesiveness and Encourage Effective Road Emergency Management Situations.

Social psychology is a branch of psychology that studies how individuals behave in social situations. The essential psycho/social element of any group is defined as a collection of people whose members influence each other in some way. Since a motorcycle club is a collection of individuals who meet to form a group, social psychological applications give us the best understanding of how to minimize riding club social problems and how to maximize the group's potential to effectively manage a bike accident if such an emergency should arise during a club ride.

In groups, "pro-social behavior" is a term used to describe how group members act in proactive, positive, and efficient ways to the benefit of the group as a whole. If an accident occurs during a club ride, clearly it is in everyone's best interest that the group behaves in a pro-social mode. In this way, the situation can be quickly managed with a minimum of chaos. Some knowledge of social psychological applications is beneficial so that if an accident happens, all members will be able to act as a well-oiled, finely-tuned machine.

One psycho/social application of particular importance for clubs to know is to rehearse and discuss possible emergency situations. In this way, all members will be able to act pro-socially, thereby avoiding the takeover of confusion and panic in an emergency. Clearly, if chaos takes over, the victim will likely not get the expedient help he or she needs. Moreover, all members will be more prone to experience psychological trauma or survivors' guilt after the accident. This would indeed be bad news and something that all riding clubs want to avoid.

If, on the other hand, all members know exactly what is expected of them in an emergency, aid for the victim(s), as well as the safety of other riders, can be managed quickly and proactively. In a pro-social situation such as this, the chances of psychological trauma to each club member will be greatly reduced. So rule number one is discuss and rehearse. This is not to suggest that members should expect an accident to happen. In fact, if motorcyclists do expect an accident to occur, this could lead to what clinicians call the "self-fulfilling prophecy" discussed earlier in the book. Since we want to avoid self-fulfilling prophesies, the club's chapter president and/or safety captain would do well to make it clear to members that discussion and rehearsal of an emergency is simply in the best interest of the group. That's all. It does not mean that an accident is inevitable.

Statistically, people are more likely to be injured or have a fatal accident in ways other than motorcycling. Let's face it: One doesn't need a motorcycle to be injured or to die. According to the book *Come Back Alive* by Robert Young Pelton, (NY, NY: Doubleday Books, 1999), in America the most frequent cause of death is heart disease. Further, you are more likely to incur injuries, accidents, or even death in your own home than anywhere else. Even athletes, such as hikers, are more likely to die from a car accident than from being in the deep woods where all sorts of mishaps can occur. For young people, the most frequent cause of death is an automobile accident. The point is, don't get stuck on the idea that you're going to be seriously injured or die because of being a motorcyclist. Countless numbers of riders live out perfectly normal life spans.

Nevertheless, motorcycling is considered a high-risk activity. Psycho/socially this means that those who engage in riding have risk-taking personality traits. This is important for riding club presidents and safety captains to know, as it often predicts what types of behaviors may take place during group rides. For example, riding in competitive ways, even if it's against group rules, can occur, because generally, motorcycle riders do have risk-taking features in their personalities. It is not bad or wrong to have risk-taking traits. In fact, most of the movers and shakers of the world have these psychological traits. Nevertheless, some knowledge of the psychology of risk-taking can help the club president, safety captain, and others to understand that noncompetitive rides should be continually encouraged at meetings. Simply having bylaws that do not allow for competition or just stating this once may not be enough.

Group competition can take on many different shapes. Often it can be in the form of unnecessary and risky riding behaviors, but it can also take the form of members trying to outdo others by purchasing bikes that are bigger, newer, and faster. It is important for the club president and safety captain to watch for behaviors that may be competitive. Signs of competitiveness may indicate certain members feel inferior in some way or feel anonymous in the group. People with risk-taking personality traits often do not like to feel anonymous or unimportant. If certain members do feel this way, the potential for membership tension, as well as the potential for ineffective functioning in a road emergency may be increased.

To counteract member competition, it is psychologically sound for club leaders to validate every member as a worthy individual and even to compliment something about each member's bike or style. In the long run, it's well worth it for leaders to take a little time at each meeting to say something validating to the group and also to say a little something special to a different individual member occasionally. Group leaders should be aware of how important their words are. Often a kind word from a leader will be remembered for a long time by an individual, even though that individual may not admit just how much it actually meant to him or her. A simple effort such as this can reduce the chances for membership competition, ultimately leading to more pro-social actions if an accident ever occurs.

If some club members are truly interested in racing and really want to compete, arrange a formal track day. This way, riding competition can be controlled in an appropriate environment at a sanctioned track school and include only those members who wish to learn proper skills for racing.

Some studies assert that the more structured a society, the more people tend to engage in risk-taking activities. Some say that the media glamorizes risk taking which may encourage some people to push themselves beyond their abilities. From a psychological perspective, risk takers and non-risk takers were once categorized into "Type A" and "Type B" personality types. Type As were thought to be adventurous, high-strung overachievers with a propensity for ulcers, heart attacks, strokes, and early deaths. More recent studies conclude that Type A and Type B categories are too general and not necessarily accurate. To correct this, researchers have coined new categories and sub-categories for risk-taking personality types.

Today the term "Type T" is used to describe risk takers. Type T has four sub-categories:

1. T-mental, for intellectual risk takers.

2. T-physical, for physical adventurers.

3. T-negative, for those with sabotaging and self-destructive physical, risk-taking behaviors.

4. T-positive, for positive and adventurous risk takers with no apparent self-destructive traits.

Type Ts are people with risk-taking personality traits. Type Ts are the movers and shaker in this world. Without Type Ts, nothing groundbreaking, revolutionary, or extraordinary would ever get done. One can imagine that Christopher Columbus and Joan of Arc must have been Type Ts.

Unfortunately, due to the stereotype of motorcyclists, many psychologists categorize riders as T-negative personalities. This is usually a false assumption and can lead a mental health worker to misdiagnose a motorcycle accident victim. In my practice I have had many clients who have seen other therapists after an accident only to be told terribly destructive and just plain ignorant things, such as, "Why on earth did you ever ride in the first place?" or "How could you even think of riding again?" So while it is good to seek psychological counseling after an accident, be very careful who you choose as your therapist. Moreover, while in a hospital for riding-related injuries, many riders are confronted by the same ignorance by nurses and doctors. Clearly, psychological and medical personnel need to be educated on the psychology of motorcyclists.

Brain chemistry reveals how thrill-seekers differ from non thrill-seekers. Norepinephrine and dopamine are neurotransmitters in the brain that affect the sensation of pleasure. Another brain chemical, serotonin, is also involved in a person's desire for thrill-seeking behaviors. EKG brain scans reveal that low-level sensation seekers tend to have high levels of the neurotransmitters norepinephrine and dopamine. For these people, small amounts of stimuli can cause high anxiety levels that can be experienced as frightening. These folks are actually scared of their own adrenaline rushes (adrenaline being another chemical involved in thrill-seeking behaviors and also in panic response). Individuals such as these are easily overstimulated and so tend to avoid motorcycles at all costs.

On the other hand, risk takers need more stimuli than non thrill-seekers to feel excitement. For these individuals, an adrenaline rush is exciting, fun, and in some cases even necessary to feel truly alive. These are the people who are adventurous. It is in their brain chemistry to be this way. Often they are rock-climbers, skydivers, skiers, and motorcyclists. Challenge is vital for thrill-seekers. This is why many riders seek out twisty, windy, mountain roads with no guardrails to protect from drops ranging from hundreds to thousands of feet below. Sounds great, doesn't it? Well, that's because we are motorcyclists. We crave a lot of stimulation. It's in our brain chemistry. To a non risk-taker, the mere idea of riding a twisty road on a bike sounds like a voyage through Hell. Risk takers do not make up the majority of the population. In fact, only about 20 percent of the populous can be considered true thrill-seekers.

Most research into group psychology involves a focus on groups that contain 3 to 20 people. Groups larger than this are known as "formal organizations."

While big group events may be exciting, they do have a tendency to diminish interpersonal social interaction, whereas smaller groups with up to 20 members tend to create more personal social contact. While many riding clubs have well over 20 members, weekly or monthly meetings are often attended by 20 or fewer riders. This means that during any given meeting, members have the opportunity to bond with each other. This is why it is common for virtually the same members to show up for regular meetings; they have bonded and, therefore, desire to see each other on a regular basis.

Studies show that groups work best when people feel that they are an important part of the whole. To encourage this, it is psycho/socially sound for clubs to give a chapter title or responsibility to individuals in order to increase their self-esteem via being an important part of the group. In other words, if given a title/responsibility, people will likely feel important due to their unique duty to the group. Usually it is up to the chapter president to initiate this idea and to encourage group discussions about it. Further, it is helpful for club leaders to learn and remember each member's name. Requiring members to wear nametags is okay at first, but this should only be used until which time the leader no longer needs them. Otherwise, people will tend to believe that the president doesn't really care who they are as individuals. Remember what we discussed earlier in this chapter: If people in a club feel anonymous, especially risk takers, this can lead to hard feelings and a loosening of group cohesion. If this occurs, those who feel anonymous may be prone to behave chaotically and be ineffective or even disruptive if an accident does happen.

Since regular attendance will vary from meeting to meeting, it is a good idea that some members are given a co-title. These people will act in the capacity of the titled person's role in case the titled individual does not attend on certain occasions. The titled and co-titled members should act in support of one another and share in the responsibility of the duties involved in their particular position. However, it is not wise for groups to elect individuals into a position that they do not want. This will only cause resentment. Psychologically, it is best to create an open dialogue to be sure each member is comfortable with the role given to him or her. Groups work best when members are comfortable with their specific title or co-title. This gives members a feeling of importance. After all, everyone wants to feel needed. It is also important that the group as a whole is comfortable with the individuals who hold specific titles and co-titles. Good old-fashioned voting can work wonders here.

Many psycho/social studies illustrate the importance of individuals understanding exactly what is expected of them in an emergency or unexpected event. These studies also teach us that relying on the help of bystanders is not a particularly good idea. One such study (Milgram, Ashe, Moriarty, "*Social Psychology*," NY, NY: Prentice-Hall, 1975) involved researchers setting up a situation whereby a woman sat on a beach while listening to a portable radio. The woman, of course, was a participant in this study. The researchers had her leave the radio unattended while she went for a swim in the ocean. Next, a man who was also part of the study stole the radio in full view of many people on the beach who were unaware of the experiment taking place. The researchers noted that only 20 percent of people who witnessed the theft of the radio made any kind of an attempt to intervene. Later, the same experiment was repeated but with a new twist. This time, the woman with the radio asked people nearby to kindly watch her radio for her while she took a swim. This time, 95 percent of the people who knew what was expected of them *did* intervene when the "theft" took place—95 percent! The point here is not that people are callous or that they don't want to help. Rather, studies indicate that individuals are far more likely to act in a pro-social way if they understand what is expected of them.

Assigning titles and co-titles is important for motorcycle groups, because individual task performance largely depends upon people having a clear understanding of what is expected of them. This is one reason why rehearsals of road emergencies are so helpful. It is also beneficial for titled and co-titled members to have their duties in writing so that there will be no miscommunication. Another reason rehearsals are important is that over time the brain builds neural tracts, or memory traces, that will come to the forefront of the brain in the event that an accident does occur.

Motorcyclists tend to be people with strong personalities. So it is best for groups to have an annual or semiannual changing of the guards. While most motorcycle clubs do this anyway, it doesn't hurt to remind and validate this to the group. In this way, the likelihood for power struggles is decreased. Membership motivation in motorcycle clubs is largely determined by cooperative agreement on group goals. Group bylaws play an important role in maintaining membership cooperation. Without bylaws and goals, the probability of group competition rises. This results in an increase of the chances for members to pit themselves against one another. Ultimately, members who are pitted against one another can reduce safety in group rides and increase the chance of chaos in an emergency.

Group cohesion largely depends upon members feeling that the group is effective in its goals. Harmony is established through open and respectful communication. Open communication has a positive effect on group morale. Leaders who gain the most respect are often those who initiate round table discussions on a scheduled basis.

Effective group communication is called "brainstorming." Brainstorming allows for open dialogue from all members and is a pro-social way to solve membership problems and social tensions. A researcher named Osborn (Osborn, A.F., *Principles and Procedures of Creative Thinking* (NY, NY: Charles Scribner's and Sons, 1957) developed important social strategies for group brainstorming. For the purposes of riding groups, I have chosen to outline only those strategies that are relevant to our pursuit of developing effective, cooperative motorcycle clubs with the goal of safety in mind. Additionally, I have modified Osborn's techniques in order to fit the psychology of motorcyclists. These techniques are as follows:

1) Inappropriate modes of criticism regarding other members should be ruled out. If people have criticisms of other members or group goals, they should speak of them in "I" terms instead of pointing fingers and blaming others. In other words, a criticism is best expressed by saying something like, "I feel angry/upset/etc. when... and I would be more comfortable if..., and what do others in the group think of my opinion?" This works much better than saying," That person did such and such, and I want that changed!"

2) Leaders do well to encourage free thinking among group members.

3) A group leader should encourage many different ideas, with all members understanding that ultimately a group vote will determine which ideas should be tried and which ones should not.

These rules allow groups to avoid being stuck in what social psychologists call, "group-consensus opinions." While it is true that group-consensus is vital to club bonding, it is also true that nothing in life is set in stone. Therefore, occasionally, group-consensus opinions can also carry the potential for clubs to be stuck in circular and worn-out ideas and behaviors. This is another good reason for clubs to have scheduled round-table discussions.

A different researcher, (Janis, 1982) developed other pro-social ways for groups to enhance the chances for positive, cooperative group cohesion. I have identified two of Janis' suggestions as most relevant to motorcycle clubs and have modified them to meet the unique needs of these groups. Janis reframed the basic idea of brainstorming into "group think." Like Osborn, Janis thought leaders must always remain objective and learn not to take issues too personally. Further, Janis asserted the importance of groups occasionally bringing in outside experts to give lectures so that clubs aren't locked into a stagnant, circular, group-consensus opinion setting that might be held onto out of habit as opposed to being beneficial to the group. Of course, lectures are not the only outside influences that can add freshness to motorcycle clubs. Encouraging members to bring in relevant motorcycle articles and books for discussion can also aid in freshening group ideas and help to prevent group stagnation. These psycho/social suggestions not only encourage group pro-social behavior but also are helpful in creating a membership cohesion that will aid in the safety of group rides as well as the group's ability to act effectively in a riding emergency (Sears, Peplau, Freedman, Taylor, *Social Psychology, 6th edition*: Saddle River. NJ: Prentice Hall, 1988, pp. 388-393).

Fear, which is the flip side of panic, has two basic components. One component is generally negative while the other is more positive. Fear is a natural reaction to a potentially life-threatening situation. In such a situation, fear is felt by both the victim and witnesses. While the victim experiences the most trauma, witnesses may experience what is called "indirect psychological trauma." In a road emergency, we want to turn the natural reaction of fear-based energy into a pro-social, proactive form of energy. The negative side of fear, which causes panic and ineffective behaviors, is an anxiety reaction that causes a lack of clear perception, a propensity to make unnecessary mistakes, and can even make one want to flee from the situation. The positive thing about fear is that it *can* be managed. In this way, the energy produced by fear can be harnessed into proactive actions.

Fear is an emotion, not a thought. Feelings have physical counterparts. Thoughts generally do not. In physical terms, fear/panic is experienced as a pounding heart, shortness of breath, sweating, and shaking. Individual differences can increase or lessen these symptoms. All of these symptoms are biochemical reactions to the emotion of fear. Recognizing these physical symptoms can help one to manage them. First, breathe deeply and slowly. Since fear causes one to breathe in a shallow manner, the brain is not able to function to its fullest capacity, because the brain needs oxygen to perform properly. Next, shake your arms and legs to give an outlet to the symptom of shaking. Now, realize that what is happening to you is natural. In this way, you will be less likely to give it too much attention. If you do not understand the natural physical reactions to fear, you will be more likely to focus on your symptoms instead of the actions you need to take in order to perform your duty for the victim and the group.

By this time (with practice, you'll be surprised just how quickly you can manage fear) you will find that the memory traces in your brain from previous discussions and rehearsals will kick in. Now you will be able to remember exactly what you are supposed to do. Moreover, the biochemical response you are experiencing can be used to provide the energy you need to behave quickly and effectively.

Motorcycle clubs should have well-defined emergency plans. These plans would include which designated member is responsible for each emergency-related duty and the best way to carry out that duty. For example, the president, vice president, safety captain, or someone else determined by the group should have a cell phone. This rider will act as the "911 Call Person." Ideally, two cell phones should be carried by two different people. Since rides often end up on out-of-the-way roads, it is important that the members who are carrying the cell phones also have a map of the route. Of course, in some cases, such as in the mountains, cell phones may not work. Therefore, the designated "911 Caller(s)" need to know the location of the nearest town with phone service.

Other designated riders in the group (or even the whole group) should be certified in first aid. Vicki Roberts Accident Scene Management class is a great way to learn what to do for a downed rider. (To learn more about Vicki's class, look for her Website.) Once again, this is where titles and co-titles come in. Titles will greatly reduce the chances for chaos in an emergency, because each person will know his or her own special duty. After all, it wouldn't help the victim much if a bunch of strong-willed motorcyclists were pushing and shoving to give aid at the same time. Most experts agree that if no one is first aid certified or otherwise medically trained, then the victim should not be touched, especially if he or she is unconscious and cannot tell you what to do for them. In this case, manage the scene around the accident and wait for the ambulance to arrive. Also, realize that if a head injury has occurred, victims may babble incoherently and sometimes even say obscene things. They don't mean what they are saying; often they don't even realize they are talking, so do not take anything said personally.

Another good idea is for someone titled or co-titled to carry road flares in order to block off oncoming motorists. And don't forget the titled "camera rider." Taking pictures of the entire accident scene can be very helpful for insurance and legal purposes. This list can go on and on. Ultimately, the club must work out for themselves what responsibilities and titles should be assigned. Fortunately, most motorcycle clubs are composed of adults who can come up with all these nuances for themselves. After all, motorcyclists tend to have risk-taking personality traits (usually T-mental and T-positive) and so can come up with plenty of great ideas. Remember, Type T people are the movers and shakers in this world.

Positive group cohesiveness and all its attendant benefits also include the club's feeling that all members are skilled riders and don't pose an unnecessary threat to the group. Club presidents and safety captains may want to determine if group rides should be segmented into units of equally skilled riders. Organizing club attendance at an advanced rider course is helpful so that members feel they are riding with the best of the best.

All too often, Americans tend to focus on the negative, such as the dangers of group riding. While it is certainly true that this is a valid issue to be addressed and managed, focusing on the positive is psychologically beneficial, too. For example, long-time riders know that there are aspects of motorcycling that can actually help to keep one safer on the road or on the dirt. Motorcycles have an amazing geometry that works quite well in terms of quick maneuverability. A skilled rider is far more agile on a bike than in a car. This can allow for the avoidance of road hazards that an automobile would not be able to miss.

Further, on a motorcycle, one has more room in a lane: the middle, left, and right channels. A car doesn't have this kind of agility. Moreover, on a bike one has far better visibility than in a car and can see what is around and what may lie ahead. Naturally, a rider must be able to handle the bike well and understand proper skills in order to make use of these potentials. But psychologically, it is sound to be aware of the benefits one has only on a bike. Your mind—your brain coupled with your personal psychology—control everything you do in life, including riding. Of course, every rider needs to be cautious and mindful of the hazards, but you can also focus on the positive. If your mind thinks of the benefits of being on a bike, your brain will scan for the safest ways to place yourself in traffic. In turn, your riding behavior will utilize the benefits inherent in the motorcycle's geometry for your personal safety. What your mind thinks is reflected in your behavior.

If an accident ever does occur in a group ride, having followed the steps outlined in this book will reduce the chances of indirect trauma to members who were witnesses to this tragic event. Nevertheless, some members may still incur some degree of indirect trauma. For example, it's not uncommon for some witnesses to question their own choices to be motorcyclists. Ultimately, making this decision should revolve around personal identity and how it is connected to being a motorcyclist. *Back in the Saddle Again* can help people experiencing indirect trauma with this issue.

Realizing that this question may come up is important, because it gives one a sense that this is a normal feeling and that others are probably questioning the same thing, even if they don't admit it. And, Type Ts often will not admit to it. Therefore, the chapter president, vice president, and safety captain would do well to have a scheduled round table discussion about the incident. Studies indicate that social support is very helpful when moving through the process of questioning and grief issues. Realize though, that Type Ts may not readily participate in such a discussion even though they really do want and need to do so.

If this is the case, one good idea is to arrange for a buddy system. One way to do this is for everyone at the club meeting to put his or her name into a helmet. Next, have members pull a name from the helmet. That name will be the "buddy" of the person who pulled it and vice versa. Buddies are there to be called upon and to generally check up on each other. A group agreement can be made whereby all buddy conversations are confidential. This way, Type Ts may feel less embarrassed by expressing their thoughts and feelings. Another suggestion is to contact the local Red Cross and arrange for a crisis counselor to come and speak to the group. Be careful with this, though. As explained earlier, some counselors do not understand motorcycling. Be sure to choose one who will not give negative comments or faulty information about riding to the club, as this may result in members feeling worse.

Assuming most members do decide to keep on riding (and most will), it is important to once again deal with the fear issue. At this time, the energy produced by fear is best turned into a new found respect for motorcycling and should be discussed in a roundtable meeting. Most clubs will find this topic is one which Type Ts may feel freer to discuss openly. To give an idea as to how fear produced by indirect trauma can be best managed, let's look at a true story of two Type T people who were involved in a life threatening boating mishap. Their story can be easily applied to motorcyclists.

In the book, *Great Survival Adventures*, compiled and edited by Robert Gannon (Random House, 1973) there is a story of a married couple who loved to take their boat into the Potomac River. Both husband and wife were Type Ts who found adventure and excitement in boating on this sometimes-hazardous river. They had been boating there for some years and felt that the thrill and beauty overrode the potential dangers. In fact, they had never been in a life-threatening situation on the Potomac, though they knew it could potentially happen. On one occasion, disaster befell them. Their beloved river suddenly seemed to turn against them. Strong currents rammed their boat into a boulder. Everything seemed out of their control. Suddenly, the currents pulled them under. Between the force of the current and their clothing weighing them down, it was nearly impossible to swim above water. Each time they popped their heads up for air, they were pulled under once again. Death seemed imminent. As Provenance would have it, fortunately these two managed to survive.

Naturally, after such an experience, the couple questioned their love of boating and of the Potomac. Eventually, they learned to turn their fear into a new respect for boating and the river. Where they had once believed that the river was somehow their friend, they now realized that the river could take on a life of its own in an instant and that nature and the Potomac were actually quite indifferent to them. They learned that the river was not actually "theirs" and that in order to boat in it, they had to develop the understanding that where there is adventure and beauty, there is also the potential for danger. This is the Yin/Yang principle of the universe. The couple did decide to boat again, but their attitude had changed. They were still able to appreciate the thrill and beauty but with a new understanding of caution and the personal responsibility one must take if a person is to live life to its fullest.

It is easy to see how motorcyclists can learn from this story. Often we do come to believe that certain roads somehow "belong" to us. That our bikes somehow "know" and are kindly disposed to us. Subconsciously, we choose bikes that represent aspects of our personality. We invest our selfhood into the bike. Motorcycles are vehicles of personal expression. We customize or hop up the engine to reflect either an existing personality feature or to represent idealized aspects of the self. But the reality is that the universe and all the objects therein are indifferent. On a conscious level, we do realize this. And so for the psychology of thrill-seekers it is because there *is* the potential of danger within the thrill and the beauty—in the magical dance between the rider, bike, and the road—that makes motorcycling so alluring.

CHAPTER 14

Debriefing

Crisis Intervention for Motorcycle Clubs
After a Road Accident

Debriefing is a psychological crisis intervention. Sometimes it is used within hours of a tragedy, but more often a psychological debriefing (P.D.) session is arranged within days, or sometimes weeks after a trauma. Generally speaking, the sooner a P.D. session can be scheduled, the better. Often, traumas are experienced and tended to by groups. If the situation warrants, debriefing can be used on one or two trauma survivors. Most often P.D. is employed in a single session format. P.D. single sessions may last anywhere from 20 minutes to two hours, depending on the type of trauma and the number of people being debriefed. For motorcycle clubs, a good half hour should be arranged for a P.D. session, with the understanding that it could last longer. However, it is a good idea to put a limit on the length of the session so that issues don't go beyond the MC (motorcycle club) debriefers' scope of training. Since a psychological diagnosis of post traumatic stress disorder (PTSD) and clinical depression can result from traumas, the purpose of P.D. is to reduce or prevent these psychological adjustment problems. This chapter is designed for motorcycle club members who witnessed a bike accident during a group ride.

Debriefing is widely used by police departments, fire-fighter units, and other Emergency Response Teams (ERT). If a motorcycle accident occurs during a club ride, usually it is the club that first tends to the accident scene. In effect, this turns the MC club into an ERT. Since formal ER Teams, such as the ones mentioned above, use P.D. as a common practice, motorcycle groups can also benefit from some knowledge of how to practically apply P.D. if a road emergency has taken place during a club ride. P.D. is an important intervention. Studies conclude that persons who have been debriefed were helped by the process and welcomed the experience.

P.D. is important for people who have witnessed a trauma even if they were not directly involved or injured by the event. P.D. helps to prevent what clinicians call "Indirect Trauma," which also can result in PTSD. Debriefing is based on a format whereby a trained facilitator opens a forum in which people are educated about the psychological effects of trauma and can safely express what they are feeling. This forum assists people to mentally organize the trauma and reduce confusion. This often decreases the chance of people developing PTSD or clinical depression.

This chapter focuses only on the basics of debriefing. First, MC clubs should appoint two debriefers who are well versed in this chapter and have discussed and planned what is outlined. It may also be helpful to do a basic Google search on a computer to learn more about P.D. However, don't overwhelm yourself with loads of information that may at times be conflicting. Clinical studies can be confusing and are really meant for mental health professionals to interpret. Since no single MC debriefer is likely to be a trained mental health clinician, having two debriefers helps a great deal. This way the responsibility can be divided so that no single individual becomes overwhelmed.

In the vast majority of cases, the basics of P.D. will be enough to assist MC clubs with post-trauma psychological adjustment. In turn, this will likely lead to a more closely-knit club, with a decreased dropout rate.

The basics of debriefing for MC clubs will be detailed later in this chapter. The following is a brief introduction to the three suggested group discussions, rules, and the four basic themes, or goals, to be addressed in a P.D. session. All the rules and themes should be presented to the group at a regularly-scheduled meeting and again at the beginning of an actual P.D. session. Group discussion rules are important after a trauma so that the session can run smoothly, with all members staying within the suggested guidelines. The sociological term "norms" refers to rules or guidelines for the meeting that the group accepts as acceptable. The format for P.D. group discussion rules is E.N.L., which in terms of norms for the discussion means

(1) EVERYONE WHO WANTS TO SPEAK SHOULD BE ALLOWED TO DO SO.

(2) NO BLAMING.

(3) LEARN FROM THE ACCIDENT.

The acronym for the four basic suggested themes or goals to be addressed is E. N.S.O.:

(1) EDUCATE: Education focuses on what types of feeling and behaviors may be expected for up to four weeks after the incident. Ideally, an MC debriefing session should be scheduled within the first week after the trauma.

117

(2)   NORMALIZE: Normalizing is an intervention whereby the MC debriefers inform club members as to what normal feelings and reactions are after a trauma.

(3)   SOCIAL SUPPORT: This chapter suggests the "buddy system" and is designed for MC clubs to be able to take care of their own tribe.

(4)   OUTREACH: Outreach is an educational process whereby MC debriefers inform the club as to what mental health resources are available in their area.

It is easy to see how these basic rules and goals of P.D. can be beneficial for motorcycle clubs. Look at it this way: if you were going to have surgery (which can be traumatic on some level for many people), you would want to know what to expect before the procedure, what will occur during the surgery, and what to expect afterwards. You would need to know what is normal and what is not. In fact, medical doctors routinely give this information to patients. This is because without this knowledge, you wouldn't have a clue as to how to prepare yourself, how to care for yourself, or how to tell if you are healing properly.

A trained crisis counselor may be best person (the Red Cross and Salvation Army can usually provide such counselors) to educate members in a meeting on the basics of P.D. Such a session can be facilitated by following the four basic steps of E.N.S.O., along with the three simple group discussion rules presented in this chapter. It is a good idea to keep things simple. Quantum physics has an acronym for this: K.I.S.S. meaning, *Keep It Simple Sweetheart.* By staying within the limits of this chapter and remembering to K.I.S.S., you can become an effective MC debriefer. If the club seems to be leading the MC debriefers out of this chapter's guidelines, remind and redirect them back to E.N.S.O. norms as well as the three group discussion rules in the "How To" section of this chapter.

MC club debriefers should let the club know that certain group rules and goals should be followed for a P.D. session, and that if some members need further assistance, they should seek individual psychological help. Let the club know that these group rules and themes are in everyone's best interest and that the most progress can be made by staying within the limits of E.N.L. and E.N.S.O. In the unlikely situation that the group as a whole seems to need additional help, a professional counselor should be asked to come in as soon as can be arranged. If this happens, it is not likely the fault of the MC debriefers, but rather an indication of the degree of trauma felt by the collective club mind.

MC club debriefers can look for certain signs that indicate that the group as a whole may be in need of a trained counselor, which include asking complicated psychological questions, appearing confused, unable to concentrate, expressing intense anger and/or irritability within the group dynamic, members blaming others or the self for what has happened, and not being able to focus on or stay within the parameters of E.N.L. and E.N.S.O. norms.

When a P.D. session is scheduled, it should always be voluntary. There should be no mandate to attend. This is because some studies suggest that for a few people, debriefing may exacerbate their issues by making them relive the trauma, for which they have no mental coping skills upon which to rely. There are a myriad of reasons as to why some folks may not currently have reliable psychological coping skills. For example, perhaps an individual has recently been through some life changes that have left them emotionally spent. MC debriefers should let the group know that everyone deserves respect, regardless if all members attend or not. Just because someone does not show up, doesn't mean that the missing member(s) don't care or are insensitive. (Indeed, hypersensitivity may be the cause!) Each individual is still a club member and should be treated as such.

After a trauma, sometimes people in groups are reluctant to open up. This may be especially true of motorcyclists and other risk takers. MC debriefers should know that jumpstarting a debriefing session filled with motorcyclists who have risk-taking personality features could require a little patience. Chances are that members are feeling confused and don't know how to express what they are feeling. After being witness to a trauma, it is not uncommon to feel a little dazed, numb, or in a state of emotional disbelief and denial at first. However, sometimes things can be just the opposite, with everyone wanting to speak at the same time. Again, outline the group rules and have members speak one at a time.

Moreover, after having witnessed an accident, many in the club may be secretly questioning if they should ride anymore. Some motorcyclists may be unwilling to freely admit this. Regardless of this inhibition, MC debriefers need to EDUCATE members that these feelings of uncertainty could surface later, and that they should get increasingly better within a four-week period of time after the accident. Also, NORMALIZE by telling the group that questioning riding is a normal first reaction for motorcyclists who have witnessed a bike trauma. Again, this feeling should pass or become increasingly better within a four-week period of time. If it does not, individuals may want to consider professional help as this could be an indication of PTSD or depression.

It is helpful for the MC debriefers to remind the club that everyone experiences life and motorcycling in a unique way. The fact that statistically an American is more likely to die from heart disease than from a bike accident may not be enough to quell the uncertainty. Occasionally, an individual may genuinely decide that he or she doesn't want to ride anymore. For some, this may be an authentic decision for which they should not be judged. *Back in the Saddle Again* can help such a person determine where this decision is coming from—if it is an authentic choice, or if it is an indication of PTSD.

In addition to the reasons cited above as to why it may be a little difficult to jumpstart a club P.D. session, remember that motorcyclists are Type T personalities, as explained in Chapter 13.

Since Type Ts may find it difficult to open up, it is important that debriefers are willing to open the dialogue by sharing their own personal feelings and thoughts first. This places a certain responsibility on the shoulders of the MC debriefers, which is why two debriefers who have discussed this material should be appointed. Elected debriefers must consider if they are willing and able to be the first to share their perceptions. This takes emotional/mental courage. Please don't accept the title of an MC debriefer if you do not honestly think you can be the first to open up. MC debriefers don't have to spill their guts, just share as many of your own perceptions with which they feel comfortable.

It's important to realize that even if you do share your perceptions first, some people in the group still may not be willing to share theirs. That's okay. Don't push it. The important thing is that now at least everyone will know what somebody else is feeling. This helps to break a sense of psychological isolation, which, in turn, helps to reduce the chance of depression. And even if members don't say anything about it, many will remember what you shared and find that in some way it was or will be, helpful for them. Realize that since people are attending on a voluntary basis, they really do want to be there, and they do appreciate the opportunity to participate in the debriefing.

Be sure to make it clear to the members who do attend the session that those who are not present still deserve the respect and camaraderie of the group. Concerning those who choose not to attend, it is a sound idea for club debriefers to give these members a phone call within several days just to let them know someone is thinking of them. It is a fairly common feeling for people who have witnessed a trauma to believe that no one understands how they feel and to perceive others as unwilling to be supportive, or to see others as uninterested. Sometimes this perception is not grounded in reality but is a trauma reaction called "perceptual distortion."

MC debriefers should be careful not to push a non-attending member to talk about his or her feelings and thoughts if the individual appears reluctant to do so. However, if after one month the member is still having adjustment problems, it may be wise to let him or her know that professional help is available to assist with a return to normalcy. Sources to find therapeutic assistance include contacting the local Red Cross, the Salvation Army, and the individual's own health insurance providers for a list of counselors in his or her area.

Sometimes when a trauma occurs, the group is neglected because the focus is on the accident victim. This is often true of motorcycle clubs. It must be remembered that no one can be expected to effectively help others if he or she has not helped him or herself. So if a bike accident happens during a club ride, after the victim is hospitalized, the group would do well to have a dual focus: support the accident victim and support each other.

It is not uncommon for a club member who has had an accident during a group ride to be besieged by membership attention for the first several days. After that, individual members sometimes find visiting the victim upsetting and may begin to either avoid the individual or to feel and act awkwardly around the injured member. Moreover, some members may feel a sort of survivors' guilt around the victim, while others may begin to see their own worst fears reflected in the eyes of the victim. P.D. is useful in reducing or eliminating the chances of this happening. Club members who support each other are better able to support the victim. Generally, members will benefit in many ways from a brief P.D. session.

If the member died as a result of an accident, have the group think in terms of a celebration of life ceremony for the person. Celebrations of life are far more psychologically sound than gloomy funerals. Life ceremonies are centered on the person as he or she lived. Funerals are all about death, which tends to create a lot of anxiety in humans. Life ceremonies reframe death into a life-affirming memory of the deceased. Take a moment, close your eyes, and compare the difference in your own mind of how you may feel after having attending a life celebration versus a death ceremony. In most cases, you will adjust more easily to the loss of your friend or loved one if the ceremony is centered on celebrating the individual's life.

HOW TO CONDUCT A MOTORCYCLE CLUB
DEBRIEFING SESSION

E.N.L.
GROUP DISCUSSION RULES
Members should be informed about these rules by the
MC debriefers.

1: EVERYONE WHO WANTS TO SPEAK SHOULD
HAVE THE OPPORTUNITY TO DO SO. This means
no interrupting. It also means that a time limit should be
set on the member's speaking. This helps members to
organize their thoughts and reduce confusion. An
average time limit could be anywhere from three to five
minutes, depending on the size of the group. Individuals
should also be allowed to speak again if time and
circumstance allow for this. MC debriefers can set a
comfortable protocol that defines a speaking procedure:
members raise their hand or stand if they wish to speak.
This protocol is a good way to avoid group confusion
and help everyone begin to mentally organize the trauma
for him or herself.

Since listening to the perceptions of others often
helps people to self-organize thoughts, speaking should
be voluntary. Each member doesn't have to share
thoughts/feelings in order to benefit from a P.D. session,
but clearly it is a good idea that at least a few members
say something about their perceptions. Remember,
though, that it may be necessary to jumpstart the group
by MC debriefers sharing their own perceptions first. On
the flip side of the coin, sometimes everyone will want to
speak at once. If this is the case, redirect everyone back
to the "no interrupting and time limit" rule. Encourage
members to organize what they want to say before
speaking. This organization of thoughts and feelings has
great psychological value. It helps the mind sort through

what an individual is experiencing internally, thereby opening the mind's "fuel valve" and allowing for the person's psychological coping skills to kick in.

2: NO BLAMING: This is an important rule. Blaming doesn't solve anything. In fact, it could even lead to membership dropout as well as increase confusion in the collective group mind. If the group or an individual member begins to blame someone for something concerning the trauma, MC debriefers can educate everyone that perfection is an "ambition," not a state of being. Also, redirect the group or blaming member to this no-blame rule and emphasize that the focus should be on what can be learned from the accident and how the group as a whole can grow from the trauma. Moreover, remind the club that a P.D. session is, in part, a forum for social support, not blame.

There can always be something said by way of support even if a member did do something wrong. We all make mistakes. Sometimes, simply a good intention is something that can be used by way of a supportive statement. And if a member did make some kind of a mistake that either caused an accident or fumbled the management of the accident scene, the club can discuss how the group as a whole may have contributed to this mistake and discuss improvements to the procedures needed. Clubs operate on the principles of group dynamics. If an individual makes a mistake, chances are that the club can benefit from learning how the group dynamic may have contributed and how to best progress and grow from there. If necessary, a vote can determine a change in a particular club rule that may have contributed to an individual mistake. But again, MC debriefers would do well to make the focus on learning, not blaming.

Naturally, in the unlikely case that some individual did maliciously cause a member to have an accident, refer to your club bylaws. This may be grounds for dismissal. If this is the case, simply give that member outreach information (detailed later) and remind them of the club bylaws for dismissal.

3: LEARN FROM THE ACCIDENT: This is a great group rule as it encourages members to think in rational terms about the trauma. This reduces what is known as "emotional reactivity"—emotionally reacting to the problem instead of rationally sorting through it. This rule is one that MC debriefers can utilize and emphasize throughout the P.D. session. It is psychologically sound for members to leave the P.D. session with information that can be learned from the accident so that the club may reduce the chances of a similar accident happening again. Keeping this focus in mind, the group may, for example, decide that the club would like to vote on breaking up rides into smaller units based on riding skill levels. An emphasis on learning is an excellent psychological focus that tends to reduce emotional reactivity in the group dynamic and encourage rational thought processes. It may be wise to wait for the next regularly-scheduled meeting to vote on any changes made so members can process the information learned from the trauma.

Additionally, to promote group cohesiveness, members should be informed that anything said in a P.D. session is confidential and to be kept within the group, with the exception of certain instances outlined later in this chapter. If members want to share information with non-attending members or family and friends, they may do so only by keeping the members, names and identifying information confidential. This ensures membership trust and encourages individuals to open up.

E.N.S.O.
All attending members should be informed of these debriefing goals.

(1)   EDUCATING: So far, you have learned that it is important that trauma survivors are educated as to what may be expected psychologically in the four weeks after the club accident. Motorcycle avoidance is a common behavior and is linked to a feeling of anxiety around riding. Questioning if riding is really worth it anymore is also common. Members should not push themselves to ride right away if they are experiencing overwhelming anxiety.

Educate that if anyone does feel a lot of anxiety about riding now, it's best to re-approach motorcycling in a step-by-step fashion. For example, read bike magazines and books, or wash and wax your bike. Sit on your bike, but don't ride. Then ride around the block until comfortable. Continue in this systematic manner until anxiety abates. These types of behaviors will allow for a gradual exposure to riding again, which is very beneficial for those who are experiencing bike avoidance. Not everyone will experience the same level of anxiety, so if a member feels that he or she can get right "back in the saddle again" with no problem, then fine. Go for it.

For survivors or witnesses of any trauma, it is not uncommon to feel that others don't understand or care about their emotions surrounding the event. This may be a perceptual distortion—a trauma reaction. MC debriefers should educate members that it is each person's responsibility to determine what type of emotional support he or she needs from family and friends and to communicate these needs. Family members and friends who were not present at the time of the accident may be at a loss as to how to help. As a result, they may become overbearing or withdrawn due to feelings of helplessness.

Since 80 percent of people are non risk takers, most people are not really able to understand what "bike-passion" is all about, and, therefore, may use an MC club accident to persuade a motorcyclist to give up riding. It's important that MC debriefers let club members know this may happen. This is part of the educational and normalizing process of P.D. If members have people in their lives who use the trauma as a way to get a rider to give up bikes, it is up to the individual to let these loved ones or friends know how they can be supportive and when personal boundaries are being violated.

Educate the club that some members may experience post-trauma nightmares or perhaps insomnia. MC debriefers should encourage members to take special care of themselves for the next month. Some suggestions include to be sure to maintain healthy eating habits and try to go to sleep at a reasonable hour; watch caffeine intake, and avoid naps to combat insomnia. Exercise is also beneficial to alleviate stress. So now would be a great time to get in physical shape! Some form of personal pampering is also a good idea. For example, arrange for a professional massage. Taking care of the self is a good way to combat depression and anxiety. Irritability may be a by-product of indirect trauma; if this is present, try to recognize it as such, and ask others to be patient with you.

Lastly, educate everyone on the normal psychological stages of grief and loss as developed by Dr. Kubler-Ross. The acronym is D.A.B.D.A.:

D: DENIAL: In the early stages of a trauma, a sense of denial, disbelief, or a numbness of feeling is normal.

A: ANGER: It is normal to feel periods of anger over what has occurred.

B: BARGAINING: This is a mental process whereby a person finds him or herself having thoughts such as, "If only I had...," or "Why did this have to happen to me?"

D: DEPRESSION: This is a normal reaction for an MC club trauma as long as it is more like the "blues" and does not reach the point where an individual feels that he or she can no longer function properly. If this state continues longer than four weeks, professional help might be needed. Remember, the P.D. session alone helps to alleviate depression. During the debriefing, be sure to include education about self-care things they can do to help prevent depression.

A: ACCEPTANCE: While the previous stages are usually overlapping and fluid (you could feel angry one day, in denial the next, and back to anger or depression), acceptance is the final stage where normal reactions come to terms with each other. At the point of acceptance, the individual has adjusted to the trauma.

(2) NORMALIZE: Normalizing is a way of reframing a perception, feeling, or reaction that a member may believe is abnormal into something normal. Often survivors wonder if their thoughts, memories, and feelings are strange and unique only to them. If this continues, it causes psychological isolation—not a good thing, folks. Normalizing during a P.D. session allows people to realize that what they are feeling, others feel too. This can do wonders for breaking a sense of

isolation, which can lead to depression. So, for example, if someone says something like, "I felt so sick to my stomach," or "I felt horrified," the debriefers may normalize these feelings and reactions by saying something like, "That sick feeling may have been your normal reaction to stress" or "I felt horrified, too." Additionally, the debriefers can ask members to share who else had a similar feeling, physical symptom, or thought. Remember here, too, that it is normal to question your own desire to ride again, at least at first.

Basically, all feelings and reactions are normal after a trauma, provided that they do not include thoughts of suicide, homicide, destruction to property, hallucinations, or other extreme and potentially dangerous feelings or reactions—and provided that they decrease and finally abate within approximately a four-week period. These extreme examples are presented only so that MC debriefers know what to look for and when it could be time to inform a family member or even the police about a member's reactions. Be sure that all members understand the circumstances under which confidentiality may be breached and that this breach is only in place to protect everyone.

When using the intervention of normalizing, it's a good idea to simply state back to the speaker what he or she has said and ask if you have heard him correctly. This reduces confusion, increases communication, and allows the individual to feel that his or her feelings have truly been heard. Remember also that when normalizing, blaming is left out of the equation, and learning from the experience is emphasized.

(3) SOCIAL SUPPORT: Club members need some emotional support from each other. One effective method of providing this to members is to set up a "buddy system." During the P.D. session, debriefers educate

members about the need for mutual support during this period. Then ask each member, including the debriefers, to write his or her name on a piece of paper, fold this, and then place into a helmet, which is passed around to every other person. (Once again, this should be a voluntary process.) Whoever's name one picks is that person's support buddy. This will be a person whom a member can call if feeling stressed about the accident or riding. (Another way to assign support buddies is by using an alphabetical match of some kind. It doesn't really matter how buddies are paired, as long as it is random, and each individual ends up with only one buddy.) If the group is oddly numbered, a debriefer may have to take on two buddies. The system will officially begin after the P.D. session and continue only until a specified date, approximately four weeks after the session, although some buddy systems continue to function on a friendly basis long after.

Very often, just knowing that a person has a support buddy is enough. Others may need to utilize the buddy system just to talk things through. There are several important aspects of the buddy system that should be made clear to all members. To begin with, all conversations must be confidential. Without confidentiality, members will not know if they can trust their support buddies. Clearly, this would be counterproductive. There is an exception to this rule, though: If, for some unusual reason, two support buddies cannot communicate effectively, or if an individual feels overwhelmed by the buddy, he or she must ask that buddy to get support from a professional or somebody else. In this situation, the overwhelmed member can breach confidentiality by informing the debriefers only.

The MC debriefers keep this information confidential and then try to provide alternate buddies, or give the problematic person(s) a list of support facilities/therapists in the area. It is also useful to learn the local crisis hotline number for your area to give people in need. This can be found in the phone book or by calling the Red Cross. If an MC debriefer is ever at a loss as to what to do, he or she can contact the local crisis hot line for help. If MC debriefers or support buddies believe that an individual is having suicidal thoughts or thoughts that could constitute a danger to self or others, they should not hesitate to contact the police, a local county mental health facility, or a family member. (This is a worst-case scenario and not likely to happen. If by a rare chance it does, at least you'll be a prepared MC debriefer.)

Support buddies should focus on mutual communication. It is important for both to share feelings about the trauma or other riding concerns. Also, it is beneficial for the buddies to establish boundaries as to appropriate times for calls.

And last but not least, MC debriefers ought to initiate a discussion about how the group can best support the accident victim. Sometimes a fundraiser is appropriate. Perhaps support buddies would like to agree to visit the individual as a team. Maybe certain members can agree upon what days they will make a visit to the victim. Some sort of agreed-upon formula greatly benefits both victim and club members. Confusion is avoided and responsibility is shared. Ultimately, everyone concerned benefits from this approach.

These are basic group rules and are a way to keep to the acronym K.I.S.S. (Keep It Simple Sweetheart). These goals and rules engender trust and help to keep boundaries that are easy to follow. It's important that no one bites off more than he or she can chew. The rules for support buddies help to ensure this. MC debriefers would do well to realize that no one can force a member to seek professional help. If things get out of hand with a certain member, MC debriefers can only provide an outreach list and then let it go. Nothing here is anyone's fault. It's just an indication of the level of trauma a particular person is experiencing.

(4) OUTREACH: Outreach is a simple P.D. goal. Prior to the session, MC debriefers should locate or create literature to be given to members which outlines mental health organizations in the general area. The phone number, e-mail, and street address of the Red Cross and Salvation Army should also be included, as these organizations offer suggestions or referrals for individuals to their own health insurance plan for counselors. Even the YWCA and YMCA often have low-fee mental health clinics. These particular mental health resources are only suggestions. Feel free to find clinics you prefer in your own area. Whatever clinics you choose, it is a good idea to find at least three and to include the local or state crisis-counseling hotline phone numbers. These hotlines are run by trained people and are often open 24/7 as well as being free of charge.

This is all it takes to run an efficient and helpful P.D. session. It's well worth it in both the short and long run to take care of your own tribe. Always remember, K.I.S.S.: Keep It Simple Sweetheart.

ABOUT
THE
AUTHOR

Brenda L Bates has a Masters of Arts degree in Counseling Psychology and is a certified hypnotherapist. Her office is in California. Among other professional specialties, Brenda holds a certificate in post traumatic stress disorder, is an athletic counselor, and is an athletic hypnotherapist specializing in motor sports. As an athletic counselor and hypnotist, Brenda also teaches seminars in sports performance enhancement from a psychological and hypnotic perspective.

Brenda is an avid motorcyclist who has been riding on-road for over 25 years and off-road for over 40 years. Within the past 10 years, she has taken up dual-sport motorcycling. Brenda holds a certificate in motorcycle engine repair which she obtained in order to be able to work on her own bikes. She is also active in animal rescue organizations. Brenda is an ardent reader with a special interest in 19th century French literature. Further, she has had a lifelong interest in the theatre and has written several plays.

Back in the Saddle Again